THE JEWISH BOOK OF WHY AND WHAT

ABOUT THE AUTHORS

Lucien Gubbay is a consulting structural engineer by profession. Saddened by widespread ignorance of the Jewish religious heritage among many Jews and non-Jews, he has long felt the need for a bridge between traditional Judaism and the general public. This book was written by him with the active help and encouragement of Abraham Levy.

Rabbi Dr Abraham Levy is the spiritual head of England's longest established synagogue–the Spanish and Portuguese Jews' Congregation, London–with the title of Communal Rabbi.

THE
JEWISH BOOK OF
WHY AND WHAT

A guide to Jewish tradition, custom, practice and belief

Lucien Gubbay and Abraham Levy

For additional information, contact:
Shapolsky Publishers, Inc.
136 West 22nd Street
New York, NY 10011

0 9 8 7 6 5 4 3 2 1

Library of Congress Cataloging-in-Publication Data

Gubbay, Lucien
   The Jewish book of why and what: a guide to Jewish tradition, custom, practice, and belief/Lucien Gubbay and Abraham Levy.
   206 p.
   Bibliography: p.
   Includes index.
   1. Judaism--Customs and practices. 2. Judaism--Doctrines.
I. Levy, Abraham, 1939- II. Title.
BM700.G833 1989   296.7'4--dc19   88-39546

ISBN 0-944007-09-0

Printed in the United States of America

An earlier edition was published in 1985 by
Darton, Longman & Todd Ltd, England
with the title Ages of Man

Contents

Preface		vii
Note on Dates		viii
Introduction		1

Part I The Ages of Man

1 Birth   9
Rejoicing – Incapacity – Priority – Circumcision – Redemption
– Naming a Girl – Visits to the Synagogue – Status of the Child

2 Bar Mitzvah and Bat Mitzvah   16
Age of Obligation – Terms – Ceremony – Bar Mitzvah – Bat
Mitzvah

3 Marriage   21
Value – Concept – Sex Drive – Polygamy – Equality of Men and
Women – Choice of a Partner – Preparation for Marriage –
Marriage Contract – Marriage Ceremony – Sex in Marriage –
Procreation and Contraception – Abortion – Divorce

4 Death and Mourning   38
The System – Care of the Dying – Arrangements for Burial –
Rending of Garments – Funeral Service and Burial – Memorial
Prayer – Kaddish – Mourning – Shivah – Sheloshim – Year of
Mourning – Memorial Stone – Anniversary – Cohen – Suicide –
Euthanasia

Part II The Framework of Belief

5 Traditional Concepts   65
Revelation – Reason – Ethics and Law – Human Life and the
World to Come – The Chosen People – The Gentiles – The
Land of Israel

6 Torah   87
Introduction – Pre-history – The Beginning – Early Midrash –
Early Mishnah – A New Beginning – Rabbi Judah's Mishnah –
The Talmud – The Geonim – Rashi and the Tosafists – The
Codes – Responsa – In Conclusion

7 Kabbalah   109
  Introduction – Early Kabbalah – Medieval Hasidism – The Zohar
  – The 'Holy Lion' – The False Messiah – East European
  Hasidism – Doctrines – Importance

Part III The Framework of Observance

8 The Jewish Year   129
  Calendar – Sabbath – New Moon – Major Festivals – Days of
  Awe – Minor Festivals and Fasts

9 The Home   144
  Daily Life – Prayer – The Family – Dietary Laws

10 The Synagogue   151
  History – The Building – Statutory Services – Structure of a
  Service – Mitzvot – Liturgy – Personnel – Synagogue Types

List of Quotations   177

Further Reading   181

Index   183

Illustrations in the Text

A Page from a Standard Edition of the Talmud   97

Development of the Torah   106

Tree of Divine Power   119

Plan of Typical Synagogue   155

Preface

This book is intended for use as a simple practical guide to Jewish practice and belief. It is not a scholarly work; and the authors are well aware that the simplification of much of the subject matter has its faults, which include lack of precision in places. Quotations are used extensively as an integral part of the text, with words and phrases not essential to the meaning being replaced by dots: for those who wish to delve further, a full list of quotations is included at the end of the book. Translations from the Hebrew are all 'free', in that both accuracy and style are sacrificed to the plain meaning of the chosen passages. The elimination of the second person singular (thee and thou) has led inevitably to some incorrect grammar. The modern or Sephardi pronunciation of Hebrew words has been used throughout, rather than the Ashkenazi. The English spelling of Hebrew words is not consistent, with the generally familiar versions preferred to the more academically correct.

The authors acknowledge with gratitude the considerable debt that they owe to their many teachers, and in particular to the late Rabbi Dr Isidore Epstein, sometime Principal of Jews' College, London.

Thanks are also due to Isaac Mozeson of Shapolsky Publishers for his valued help in preparing the American edition of this book.

LUCIEN GUBBAY
ABRAHAM LEVY

Note on Dates

Dates in general use are given in the Jewish style in the text. B.C.E. (BEFORE COMMON ERA) is equivalent to B.C. (BEFORE CHRIST); and C.E. (COMMON ERA) corresponds to A.D. (ANNO DOMINI). For example:

$$165 \text{ B.C.E.} \quad = \quad 165 \text{ B.C.}$$
$$1380 \text{ C.E.} \quad = \quad \text{A.D. } 1380$$

The numbering of years since creation, in accordance with the Jewish religious calendar, is explained in chapter eight.

Introduction

How goodly are your tents, O Jacob, your dwelling places,
Israel, like long rows of palms, like gardens by the
river . . .[1]

The above words were uttered by the gentile prophet Balaam,
when called upon to pronounce a curse on Israel. Standing
on a mountain top overlooking the multitude of the people,
Balaam could find no fault.

These days, even to a sympathetic observer, traditional
Judaism can often present aspects at once bewildering and
forbidding. Many of its customs and habits are cloaked in
the alien manners of originally immigrant communities: the
impact of its prayers and writings are veiled by the use of the
Hebrew tongue: the almost ostentatious warmth of the family
and social life of its adherents can seem inward-looking and
exclusive. Against a cultural background influenced by
classical, by Christian and by humanist traditions, knowledge
of Judaism is hard to come by, even for Jews themselves;
misconceptions and misunderstandings flourish uncorrected.

A common view of the Jewish faith held by otherwise well-
educated outsiders can best be summed up in the very words
chosen to describe the scriptures in the English language: Old
Testament and New Testament. The Old Testament is often
regarded as an outmoded religious text of certain limited
historical interest, embodying the beliefs of a narrow sect.
The New Testament on the other hand is represented as the
final distillation of the crude 'old' revelation, containing a
universal message for all mankind. The knowledgable reader
may well gasp with incredulity on first hearing this
contemptuous dismissal of the rich and complex body of
Jewish teaching; but should understand that views of this

1

kind are widely held, and by no means restricted to the ill-intentioned. Many centuries of active Church hostility in early and medieval times have certainly left their mark on contemporary awareness and attitudes. Indeed, as now portrayed by popular education, by the press, radio and television, Judaism seems to have few attractions to pit against those of the Church. The unschooled have no means with which to compare the merits of the original Hebrew Bible with the sheer beauty of the King James version: the informality and disorder of many synagogue services appear uncouth beside the liturgical and musical cadences of the Church, with the direct Christian debt to Jewish words and forms of prayer both unperceived and unacknowledged: the foreign accents of many traditional rabbis can grate in comparison with the more polished speech of their clerical counterparts; and what may be even more significant, where major works of Jewish learning do exist in English translation – such as the Talmud – their structures are so unlike those of other religious writings as to render them incomprehensible to the ordinary reader without the help of skilled teachers and interpreters.

It is not always realised that increasing numbers of Jews themselves have become almost as alienated from the religious heritage of their own people as are their gentile neighbours. It is easily done – a scanty religious education in some cases, one generation of religious non-observance in others – and individuals rapidly evolve who, though proud of being Jewish in some obscure way, are almost innocent of the practices and beliefs of their more indentifying brethren, and this despite occasional attendance at a place of worship, or even nominal membership of a synagogue or temple. The authors of this guide have often been struck by the plight of such people, suddenly confronted with religion when they are at their most vulnerable – at the death of a loved one, for example; and have been moved by their embarrassment and frustration in then having to cope with a tradition only dimly comprehended, and whose content may seem to consist of little more than a series of ritual formulae, empty of real meaning and compassion. It is partly for them that this book is written, in the hope that for some at least it may provide a first step towards understanding that body of observance developed throughout the ages for their guidance and comfort. If it leads to further efforts to learn more about that sublime edifice of Divine inspiration and human achievement commonly described as Judaism, the authors will be amply rewarded. They believe that once the initial barrier is overcome, further and deeper study may become more attractive; and that a Jew's closer approach to his Creator, through the traditional wisdom of his people, can be life-enhancing to a degree yet unsuspected.

Part I aims to provide an account of Jewish custom and practice surrounding the major landmarks in life, in a manner easy to understand by those with little or no knowledge of Jewish ways. It is complete in itself and may be consulted or read on its own, without reference to what follows. As awareness of death often prompts the initial impulse towards religion, this is dealt with in more detail than the chapters on marriage, coming of age, and birth. However, no such account can be complete without mention of the Jewish concept of God and creation, and of the formal structure of the faith – in other words, 'The Framework of Belief' (Part II): here the authors' task bristles with difficulty – how to avoid writing yet another elementary textbook on Judaism, how to compress within relatively few pages the wisdom accumulated by countless generations of saints, sages and scholars. At the risk of superficiality, the authors have limited themselves to describing only the barest outlines of thought and belief. Their work contains no original ideas or research: it relies heavily on the writings of others, its sole intention being to provide a simple key to one door in that facade of unfamiliarity, behind which lies a whole world awaiting discovery by many who could benefit from its awareness. The last section, Part III, 'The Framework of Observance', is also reasonably self-contained; and endeavours to cover the day to day observances of practising Jews in their homes and in their places of worship.

Until the early years of this century Jews were to be found living in most inhabited parts of the earth – from the edges of the Asian steppe to the countries of western Europe, from the remote emptiness of lands like the Yemen to centers of international trade in India and China, and also in North and South America and in Africa. It is hardly surprising therefore that the mantle of Judaism should cover a rich diversity of habit and ritual. The first and simplest division to be made is that between Ashkenazim and Sephardim. Ashkenazim, originally meaning Jews of German origin – but generally taken to include most Jews from northern France, Germany central and eastern Europe – had their traditions first formed in the hostile cramped environment of Palestine under Roman occupation, and later developed under the harshly repressive regimes of medieval Christianity. Sephardim, originally meaning Jews of Spanish origin – but generally taken to include most Jews from the Mediterranean basin and the Near East – forged their early traditions in the comparatively free and prosperous environment of the first great community of exiles in Babylon, and developed them under the sometimes sympathetic and tolerant, and sometimes persecuting regimes of Islam. Rather surprisingly, for people who lived apart for so long, only relatively unimportant differences are now apparent between Ashkenazim and Sephardim in England and the United States, mainly in their prayer books, synagogue music, Hebrew pronunciation, and in some customs deriving from their countries of origin.

The other main divisions between Jews are connected to the way in which they interpret the requirements of their faith – for sincere Jews practice their religion in a variety of ways, some of which differ appreciably from the traditionally orthodox approach. Members of contemporary Hasidic sects, and those loosely described as 'ultra-Orthodox', positively reject any idea of synthesis between the secular (non-Jewish) world and that of religion. For them the generally accepted standard of religious observance is much too low, and they aim to lead lives of intense and conspicuous devotion. On the other hand, by rationalizing and thus to some extent diluting traditional ways, the followers of Progressive Judaism go further towards accommodating the outside world than is acceptable to the majority of traditionalists.

In the Reform and similar movements, Jews have tried to overcome barriers to acceptance and understanding by moving their religion closer to the contemporary thought and experience of the largely non-Jewish environment in which they live. They do not fully accept the belief, crucial to traditionally orthodox Jews, that the Torah (the first five books of the Bible, the Five Books of Moses) is wholly of divine origin;

and they also partly disregard the authority of past generations of rabbis who developed the Halacha (traditional Jewish
law and practice). Conservative Judaism, which attracts widespread support in the United States, accepts the validity of
the Halacha, but then adopts a much more innovative approach to Jewish law than that of traditional Judaism.
Though much mutual antagonism has been generated by the
tragic division within Judaism between those who accept the
full authority of the Halacha and those who do not – the
traditionalists (or 'orthodox') and the progressives – recent
trends within Reform, Conservative and Reconstructionist
Judaism demonstrate a growing respect for traditional practice, if not belief.

Detailed accounts of the differing customs and beliefs of
the principal groups on either side of mainstream traditional
Judaism must necessarily lie beyond the scope of this brief
guide. The fuller explanations given here are based on the
centrist form of traditional Judaism represented by such bod-
ies as the Rabbinical Council of America, the United Synagogue of London and the Spanish and Portuguese Synagogues of New York and London, but reference is also made
to Reform customs and practice where these vary appreciably.

Though the explanations given in this book are couched in
simple terms, it is hoped that no one will fall into the error
of thinking that Jewish religious thought and experience are
necessarily equally simple. The great problems of the nature
and purpose of existence have occupied many profound minds
since the beginning of history; and Jews have played a full
part in this activity. The traditional delight of rabbis is to
explore every possible interpretation of the meaning of a single
phrase from the Bible for hours on end – which activity is
itself regarded as a form of religious service – and numerous
volumes are devoted to the elucidation of more difficult passages. Religious truth exists on many different levels of
understanding, from that of the uneducated layman to that of
the accomplished scholar. Likewise religious thought is also
capable of expression in different ways, ranging from the
lucid utterance of the philosopher to and beyond the limit of
articulation of the most sublime mystic. On the surface Judaism presents a rational and straightforward front: study of
mysticism is restricted to small circles of the initiated, and

dabbling by the relatively ignorant is not encouraged. Mystical practice is even more severely discouraged; and the story is told in the Talmud of the four great sages who penetrated the mystic realm – Simon ben Azzai died, Simon ben Zoma went mad, Elisha ben Aruyah gave up Judaism and became an apostate, and only Rabbi Akiva returned to this world unscathed by his experience. However it must not be forgotten that mystical doctrines known as Kabbalah (tradition) have existed within Judaism from the time of the second Temple to the present day. Beside and behind every simple explanation given in this guide, there are layers of meaning; and these include those based on speculation concerning the hidden bridges over that abyss which separates the finite world in which man lives from the infinite towards which he yearns.

The words of the opening passage of the Book of Jeremiah have been chosen to conclude this introduction. In the strikingly beautiful image of a young bride following her husband through a harsh and stony landscape, the Lord recalls the closeness to God of previous generations of the House of Israel:

> I remember the unfailing devotion of your youth, the love of your bridal days, when you followed me in the wilderness, through a land that was not sown.[2]

May those days be renewed, for each one of us, in our separate ways.

Part I

The Ages of Man

1

Birth

REJOICING

The wonder and joy experienced by most people in the world on the birth of a child is shared in full by Jews, who celebrate the beginning of a new life with high emotion.

The first command given to man in the Bible is 'Be fruitful and multiply'. In the Jewish tradition life is regarded as a precious gift from God, to be treasured above almost all else. Religion therefore can add yet another dimension to natural human feelings.

INCAPACITY

The inability to bear children has always been considered a grievous misfortune, and the Bible contains several poignant accounts of the suffering endured by barren women.

Adoption is an acceptable way of satisfying the deeply felt need of many childless couples for children, and of children for the love and security of family life. Non-Jewish children may be converted to Judaism for this specific purpose.

Modern Jewish law permits the artificial impregnation of a wife with her husband's sperm (A.I.H.). Artificial insemination by a donor (A.I.D.) is objected to by the Rabbis, mostly on the grounds that the hidden identity of the donor implies a risk that 'children' of the same father may meet in later life, and then form incestuous relationships.

The 'in-vitro' fertilization of a wife's ovum with her husband's sperm is permissible, while the same objections as those advanced against A.I.D. apply to cases in which the donors are not husband and wife.

9

Many moral and legal problems have been raised by the difficult question of surrogate motherhood; and rabbinic opinion has now crystallised firmly against the use of a surrogate mother in any circumstances.

PRIORITY

In Jewish law an infant is not considered to have the full status of a human being until the larger part of its body (or its full head) has emerged from that of its mother. Before that moment the preservation of the mother's life is paramount in any emergency; and if necessary the baby must be sacrificed to save the mother.

BERIT MILAH (Covenant of Circumcision)

> Every male among you shall be circumcised . . . in the flesh of your foreskin; and it shall be a token of a covenant between Me and you . . . he that is eight days old shall be circumcised. . . .[1]

Circumcision was not invented by the Jews, and probably dates back to prehistoric times. Abraham circumcised himself in his old age, in obedience to God's command, as a token of the covenant; and since then the rite has assumed great significance for Jews. The children of Israel were circumcised by Joshua before entering the Promised Land, for the practice had been discontinued during the rigours of the long march through the wilderness. When the institution lapsed again during the reign of King Ahab and Queen Jezebel (874–852 B.C.E.), it was triumphantly revived by the Prophet Elijah, who thus earned himself a place in all future circumcision ceremonies.

The proscription of BERIT MILAH by the Emperor Hadrian was one of the causes of Bar Kochba's revolt against Roman rule in 132–135 C.E; and many Jews throughout the ages have faced martyrdom rather than forgo this sacred obligation. Spinoza declared: 'Such great importance do I attach to this sign of the covenant, that I am persuaded that it is sufficient in itself to maintain the separate existence of the Jewish people for ever.'[2]

When a Roman official, questioning the attachment to circumcision, asked Rabbi Oshaya why God had not made man as he wanted him the reply was given that it was in order that man should have the opportunity of perfecting himself by the fulfilment of a Divine command. Many other semi-rational arguments have been advanced for the necessity of circumcision, mostly to do with the health of the male, the health of the female partner, and with sexual satisfaction. However, the TORAH (teaching, or law) troubles itself not with any of them: it states firmly that circumcision is the visible sign of that special relationship between the Jewish people and their God, by means of which the Divine message was transmitted for the benefit of all mankind.

Thus, after seeing to the needs of the mother and infant son, the happy father's first task is to arrange for the Berit (covenant). It is the father's duty to do so; and should he fail, a Jewish court (BETH DIN) will act for him. Circumcision is not a sacrament; and any child born of a Jewish mother is Jewish whether circumcised or not. The rite must be performed on the eighth day after birth, even on a Sabbath or on the Day of Atonement; and this is considered to be so important that the infant's health is the only valid reason for delay.

The local synagogue will be able to recommend a qualified MOHEL to perform the operation. It should be realized that the Mohel, though usually not a doctor, is highly skilled and rigorously trained for his task: he carries out so many of these operations that he will very often be far more dextrous than an ordinary medical practitioner. Some people may prefer to have the rite performed by a Jewish doctor who is also a qualified Mohel, and this can often be arranged. The Mohel must be Jewish, and religiously observant.

The ceremony may be carried out at home or in the hospital. At least ten Jewish males to form a quorum (MINYAN) should be present. A special chair is prepared in honour of the Prophet Elijah, who is considered to be the protector of the child because of his restoration of the rite in the time of King Ahab: Ashkenazim place the child on the chair for a moment or two; whilst, in the Sephardi tradition, the SANDAK (father's companion) occupies the seat. As it is the father's duty to carry out the circumcision if competent to do so, he must authorise the Mohel to act on his behalf. Immediately after the operation the father recites the following blessing:

> Blessed are you O Lord our God, King of the universe, who has sanctified us by your commandments and commanded us to initiate this child into the covenant of our father Abraham.

Sephardim add a further blessing to God: '. . . who has kept us alive, sustained us and enabled us to reach this season.'

The Sandak holds the child firmly on his lap for the duration of the operation. If still living, one of the child's grandfathers is usually asked to act as Sandak, which is considered to be a great honour. The comparatively modern association of 'godfather' with the role of the Sandak owes a good deal to outside influences.

A special KIDDUSH (prayer of sanctification) is then pronounced over wine; and the child is given his Hebrew name. Naming customs vary a great deal in different Jewish communities: some will name a child after a living grandparent: others will not do so if the grandparent is still alive, and will name the child only after the dead. Relatives can be very sensitive in the matter of bestowing a name; and the Rabbi should always be consulted in case of doubt.

A festive meal or other celebration usually follows the ceremony of Berit Milah.

REDEMPTION (Pidyon Ha-ben)

Firstborn males enjoyed many privileges in the ancient world. In the Jewish tradition the firstborn belong to God's service. They were intended originally to serve in the sanctuary; but lost that honour to the Levites after the Israelites turned aside from God in the desert of Sinai to worship the golden calf.

Apart from children of the hereditary priestly families (Cohen) and the hereditary Levitical families (Levy), every such boy must therefore be redeemed by his father from the priests. The child of a woman whose father is a priest or Levite is also exempt from the obligation. No redemption is required for a child born of a Caesarean operation, or after his mother had a previous miscarriage – he must be 'firstborn of the womb' to need redeeming.

The ceremony, which is a short one, takes place on the thirty-first day after birth, unless this is a Sabbath or festival. A COHEN regarded by tradition as a descendant of the family of Aaron the High Priest, asks the father whether he wishes to redeem the child, or leave him with the priest. The father expresses his desire to keep the child; and hands the priest five coins of large denomination, symbolic of the five shekels specified in the Bible. The father then pronounces a blessing of thanksgiving for having been enabled to fulfill the commandment of redemption; and the Cohen returns the child to his father, saying three times, 'Your son is redeemed.' The Cohen will then bless the child with the priestly benediction:

May the Lord bless you and keep you.
May the Lord cause His face to shine upon you and be gracious unto you.
May the Lord look kindly on you and give you peace.[3]

It is customary for the Cohen to give the redemption money to charity.

The ceremony is often followed by a celebration.

NAMING A GIRL

A girl is usually named in the synagogue when the father is called to the reading of the Torah on his first visit after the birth. Another custom, more usual amongst Sephardim, is for the girl to be named in a little ceremony on the mother's first visit to synagogue after the birth, to give thanks for her safe delivery. In yet another tradition a girl is named in a ceremony held in the home on a Sabbath morning.

The ceremony is brief, and consists of a simple prayer for the child's health, and for a life of joy, fulfilment in marriage, riches and honour. She is named as follows: 'May He who blessed Sarah, Rebecca, Rachel and Leah . . . bless this beloved child, and may her name be_____'

VISITS TO THE SYNAGOGUE

The father should visit the synagogue on the Sabbath following the birth of his child, when he will be called to the reading of the Torah in honor of the occasion. The title

AVI HA-BEN (father of a newborn boy), or
AVI HA-BAT (father of a newborn girl), or
BAAL HA-BERIT (master of the covenant), if the circumcision has taken place that day,

is added after his name, as appropriate so that those present can mark the event and join in the rejoicing.

The mother should also visit the synagogue, either alone or with the baby, at a time when no public service is being held. On the steps of the Ark, she will thank God for his great blessing:

Blessed are You, O Lord our God, King of the Universe, who grants benefits to the undeserving; for You have granted me only good.

A baby girl can be named either by the father or by the mother during their visits to the synagogue on the above occasions.

STATUS OF THE CHILD

Jewish law regarding the religion of a newly born child is simple. A child is Jewish if born of a Jewish mother: the father's standing is not relevant, and no other consideration applies.

Thus the child of a Jewish father and a non-Jewish mother is not Jewish; and the child of a non-Jewish father and a Jewish mother is Jewish. A female convert to traditional Judaism is regarded as Jewish in all respects, including the ability to pass on that status to her children. Trouble sometimes arises in connection with women who have been converted to Judaism by one of the so-called progressive Jewish organisations: as such converts are not recognised as

Jewish by the orthodox authorities, their children are also regarded by them as non-Jews.

Illegitimacy, in so far as this applies to children born out of wedlock, is not a Jewish concept, and has no meaning in Judaism.

It is, however, sad to have to relate that Jewish law contains a far sterner concept – that of the MAMZER (incorrectly translated as 'bastard'). A mamzer is the offspring of a forbidden relationship, that is an incestuous union, or one between a married woman and a man other than her husband. A mamzer is prejudiced in only one way, but that is a grievous one – he or she is only permitted to marry another mamzer or a convert. That however provides little relief, for a child of such a marriage is also a mamzer. It is small consolation to note that a mamzer who is a scholar would take precedence over a High Priest who is an ignoramus, for problems caused by the status of the mamzer are among the most difficult and disturbing that ever come to the attention of the Rabbis.

2

Bar Mitzvah and Bat Mitzvah

AGE OF OBLIGATION

The tender ages of thirteen for a boy and twelve for a girl are those at which, in Jewish law, a child assumes the full moral and legal responsibilities of an adult. These ages, representing the onset of physical maturity, relate originally to the distant past. The Rabbis teach that both Abraham and Jacob made crucial decisions governing the future conduct of their lives at the age of thirteen – Abraham abandoned the idol worship of his father, and Jacob parted from Esau.

To view the traditional age of majority in historical perspective, it should be remembered that the first modern attempt to control the abuse of child labour in mines and factories was passed by the English parliament only in 1802, and then proved ineffective; and also that children, often as young as seven, still constitute up to a tenth of the total labour force of many countries of Asia, Latin America and the Middle East.

From the age of thirteen years and one day, a father is no longer responsible for the actions of his son. The boy is then considered an adult in law: he is eligible to form part of a MINYAN (quorum of ten adult males required for the holding of a public religious service): with very few exceptions, he is able to engage in legally valid transactions for which he is held to be fully accountable.

A girl is, in theory, able to marry at the age of twelve years and one day. This now has a significance that is more historic than real; for even in Israel, where religious law governs the personal status of Jews, a girl is not normally permitted to marry under the age of seventeen.

TERMS

The terms BAR MITZVAH (son of the commandment) and BAT MITZVAH (daughter of the commandment) are used in two ways. The first is to describe the state of adulthood entered into at the age of thirteen for a boy and twelve for a girl; and the second is the name of the ceremony and celebration accompanying the attaining of those ages.

Contrary to popular belief, no ceremony of any kind is necessary. All Jewish children automatically become Bar Mitzvah or Bat Mitzvah at the appropriate age, even if they are entirely unaware of that fact. The lack of a ceremony to mark the event may well leave a person with a feeling of deprivation; but it has no more significance than that. When adult members of temples arrange a Bar Mitzvah or Bat Mitzvah ceremony for themselves to make up for one missed in youth, they are fulfilling a deeply-felt personal need, and not a requirement of Jewish law or tradition.

CEREMONY

Though completely unknown before the fifteenth century, the custom of celebrating a boy's attaining the age of Bar Mitzvah has assumed great importance in Jewish family life. The boy will study hard for his performance in synagogue on the great day; and the subsequent festivities can sometimes equal those for a wedding in their scale, and in the feelings of joy and pride that are aroused.

The custom of celebrating a girl's becoming Bat Mitzvah is of even more recent origin, and dates back only to the nineteenth century. Some parents will merely treat the event as a rather special birthday; but others will use it to demonstrate their love for their daughter. As women do not take part in the ceremonial of traditional synagogue services, a girl's performance is necessarily very limited. Non-traditional congregations, having no restriction on the participation of women, give girls and boys equal treatment.

BAR MITZVAH

Jewish men are required by biblical law to wear TEFILLIN during morning prayers. These are small boxes containing the written words of the SHEMA ('Hear O Israel, the Lord is our God, the Lord is one...'), one of which is strapped to the forehead and the other to the left arm (except for a left-handed person). Jewish men may also be 'called' to the public reading of the Torah (Five Books of Moses; the first five books of the Bible) in the Synagogue.

The Bar Mitzvah ceremony, as it has developed, concentrates on the boy's new obligations as a man. On the Monday or Thursday following his thirteenth birthday in the Jewish calendar (*not* the secular calendar: see chapter eight) he will attend morning service in the synagogue. There he will put on Tefillin for the first time; and then will be called to the reading of the Torah. Unlike ordinary worshippers whose portion is read out for them by the designated Reader, the boy will have the duty of reading his own portion. A Monday or Thursday is usually chosen, for it is only on those days that the Torah is read during the morning service – except for the Sabbath, when Tefillin are not worn. This, in some Jewish communities, *is* the Bar Mitzvah: in most others it is either omitted altogether or else is followed by a more public ceremony on the following Sabbath.

In what is now commonly understood as the Bar Mitzvah service, family and friends are invited to the Sabbath morning service in the synagogue: the father and other male members of the family will be allotted MITZVOT, which are honored roles in the ceremonial (see chapter ten). The Bar Mitzvah will be called to the reading of the Torah; and will often sing his own portion with some display of virtuosity. A boy with ability may also read the other portions, the HAFTARAH (portion from the Prophets) or other parts of the service, depending on local custom. The Rabbi will address the boy in a sermon, stressing his new responsibilities as a full member of the Jewish community. In some synagogues the boy also recites a special prayer affirming his devotion to the faith of his ancestors.

A modern Bar Mitzvah celebration is a great occasion; and the boy will receive gifts from all those invited to it. It is customary for the boy to deliver a DERASHAH (scholarly lecture) during the festive meal; and even when this is not done the boy will still make a speech in which he thanks his parents, family and teachers for their love and care.

Many comparatively non-observant Jewish families also celebrate the Bar Mitzvah of a son in the manner described above. This is useful in that the occasion, and the preparation for it, serves to bring the child and his parents a little closer to the synagogue, if only for a short time. However there can be negative aspects, particularly in the educational sphere. If a child attends religion classes primarily to enable him to perform well in the synagogue on the day of his Bar Mitzvah, and a large part of his learning consists of preparing to sing the chosen Hebrew passages, and he then leaves promptly on attaining 'manhood' at the age of thirteen – then he will emerge from the educational process with very little knowledge indeed. The vital importance of a well-balanced, thorough and sustained religious education cannot be stressed too often: it far outweighs the value of a single star performance one morning at the age of thirteen. Jewish living should start, not end, at Bar Mitzvah or Bat Mitzvah.

BAT MITZVAH

One form of Bat Mitzvah ceremony in a traditional synagogue is for the girl to give a short discourse on the weekly portion from the Torah (the first five books of the Bible). This takes place on a Saturday morning, after the conclusion of the morning service (Musaf).

Another way of celebrating a girl's Bat Mitzvah in a traditional synagogue it to arrange a special service, sometimes on a Sunday afternoon, in which several girls might participate together. Relatives and friends are invited. Psalms and other prayers are recited by the girls; and a sermon is preached to them. Proceedings usually end with the invocation of the priestly blessing on the girls:

May the Lord bless you and keep you.
May the Lord cause His face to shine upon you and be gracious unto you.
May the Lord look kindly on you and give you peace.[1]

The Bat Mitzvah ceremony in a Reform temple is identical to the Bar Mitzvah ceremony of a boy.

Festivities will follow the synagogue service; and the girl will receive gifts from all the guests. Though the celebrations are often smaller in scale than those for a Bar Mitzvah, most sensitive parents will ensure that their daughter does not feel that she is undervalued in any way: the role of a woman is different from that of a man in traditional Judaism, but it is certainly not inferior.

3

Marriage

VALUE OF MARRIAGE

It is not good for man to be alone. I will provide a partner for him . . . a man leaves his father and mother and is united to his wife, and the two become one flesh.[1]

The institution of marriage is one of the pillars of Judaism, considered essential for the preservation of society. The Rabbis view the married state so highly that they use that analogy to illustrate the significance of many of the most important combinations in Jewish life. God is said to be 'married' symbolically to the Jewish people: the Jews are said to have contracted a 'marriage' with their Torah; and the Sabbath is regarded as the 'bride' of the Jewish people, as expressed by the hymn sung on Friday evenings to greet its onset:

Come my beloved to meet the bride; let us welcome the presence of the Sabbath.[2]

Marriage was established by Divine law. Conduct within a marriage, and rules for its dissolution are regulated by Divine law. A person is not fulfilled until married; and celibacy of any kind is strongly discouraged by traditional Judaism.

CONCEPT OF MARRIAGE

The Jewish attitude to marriage differs decisively from that of the Catholic Church, and from that of modern secular society. Jews have never regarded marriage as a concession to man in order to cope with his sinful sexual instincts – on the contrary, within limits, sex is regarded as an essential ingredient of a complete life. Jews have never regarded marriage as a sacrament, indissoluble except through the death of one of the partners – a Jewish divorce, if by mutual consent, is always available. Jews have never regarded marriage as an experimental association between two people, free to make up rules to suit themselves as they go along – Divine law regulates conduct within marriage. Consequently a Jewish marriage is different in concept, and perhaps even in quality, from one entered into under other laws and in other societies.

From a technical point of view a Jewish marriage is a simple contract between two people, imposing obligations on both and specifying conditions to be met in the event of breakdown. If both parties agree, a divorce can be effected by a simple legal ceremony, after which they are each free to remarry at will.

However since earliest times the plain legal aspect of the marriage union has acquired overtones of holiness. Many rabbinic legends refer to God's interest and approval in the making of marriages; and we read that the Divine altar in heaven 'sheds tears' at the news of a divorce. Marriage therefore is not merely a cold legal arrangement; but is also a holy institution, blessed by God.

SEX DRIVE

Mankind has developed widely differing attitudes towards basic human instincts such as sex, eating, drinking, and the acquisition of wealth and power. On the one hand the old pagan world often gloried in satisfying some appetites: Romans would gorge themselves with food and then induce vomiting so that they could gorge themselves all over again: the Semitic word for a 'prostitute' has the same root as the word for 'holy', illustrating the fact that prostitutes once practiced their trade in the precincts of idolatrous temples. The early Church, on the hand, together with aberrant Jewish sects such as the Essenes, regarded sex as sinful and urged celibacy instead. Food and drink were consumed only in sufficient quantities to ensure physical survival; power and wealth were scorned in favor of what was thought to be the ideal life of poverty, chastity and obedience.

Both of these extremes are unacceptable to Judaism, which teaches the lofty ideal of 'Make yourself holy with that which is permitted to you'.[3] In other words, most human instincts are neither to be suppressed, nor glorified. Instead they are to be indulged in moderation, with self-discipline, so that they may be consecrated to God. This is the reasoning behind the elaborate Jewish laws concerning the preparation and consumption of food (KASHRUT), and those concerning the channelling of the sex drive.

Were it not for the sexual instinct,
no man would build a house,
marry a wife or beget children.[4]

The above quotation from the Talmud is a good example of the Rabbis' thinking on the subject. Sexual relations are an essential part of marriage, and their denial is a prime ground for divorce. The marriage contract itself specifically refers to the obligation to maintain a full and regular sex life. Conjugal rights for women were included in Biblical legislation long before the days of modern feminism.

POLYGAMY

Polygamy was not forbidden by the Torah, and the Bible includes many instances of men who had more than one wife. In practice, however, Jewish society had become almost completely monogamous by Talmudic times. In the tenth century polygamous unions were absolutely forbidden to all Ashkenazim by Rabbi Gershon. This prohibition gained widespread acceptance by Sephardim too, even though the practice of polygamy was normal in Moslem lands in which most were living. It is interesting to note that even amongst those few Sephardim who did allow polygamy, their marriage contracts stipulated that a husband could only undertake a second marriage with the express permission of his first wife. In modern Israel, where Jewish law governs family and personal matters, polygamy is forbidden.

EQUALITY OF MEN AND WOMEN

The commonly held fallacy that a Jewish husband 'acquires' a wife, as he might acquire a chattel, is based on total misunderstanding of Jewish law and practice. Though the man is the actual instigator of the making and of the breaking of a marriage contract, the full force of Jewish law is directed towards the protection of the woman's rights, both in marriage and subsequently.

It must be remembered that Jewish marriage laws were framed and developed at a time when wives in general had few rights. For example, though a married woman has always been allowed to own property in her own right in Jewish law, this was not possible in England until the passing of the Married Women's Property Act about one hundred years ago.

The marriage contract had two main purposes – the first was to guarantee the material, social and sexual rights of the woman during the marriage; the other, connected with the marriage settlement, was to protect the woman's financial position in the event of a divorce or the death of her husband. The settlement itself is a specific sum of money which the husband is legally obliged to hand over to his wife in case of divorce, and it is the first charge on the husband's estate on death.

Divorce is easy, if by mutual consent. In law, the husband prepares the GET (bill of divorce), and the wife accepts it in a simple ceremony. Should the woman refuse to accept the Get, the man can appeal to the court (BETH DIN) for assistance. Should a husband refuse to grant a divorce, then no divorce is possible – and it is this aspect that is often criticized today. In Jewish society great moral and social pressure is exerted by rabbis on an unreasonable husband who refuses to grant a divorce. In Israel, where religious law is paramount in such matters, rabbinical courts have been known to impose sanctions on a recalcitrant husband until he agrees to deliver the required bill of divorce to his wife. Jews consider their law to be God-given and immutable. It can often be reinterpreted to suit altered conditions at different times, but as the actual clause states that it is the man who delivers the bill of divorce to the woman, the Rabbis still find themselves unable to sanction any basic alteration, despite the hardship that can be caused in some cases and the many criticisms of unfairness from some sections of society. However, all that can be done to help in cases of difficulty is done, without actually breaking the letter of the law.

The status of the Jewish woman in marriage and in the home is long-established and unassailable: 'Who can find a capable wife for her worth is far above rubies. Her husband's whole trust is in her. . . . She is clothed in dignity and power. . . .'[5]

The parody of the strong Jewish mother, repeatedly portrayed with such humor in modern American fiction, is nevertheless firmly based on the age-old concept of the vital importance of the woman's role as a full partner in the marriage.

CHOICE OF A PARTNER

Hasten to buy land, but deliberate long before taking a wife.

The Rabbis were fond of giving what they considered to be sound practical advice about choosing a marriage partner: respectability of family, and similarity of social background were (and still are) important considerations. Views such as 'Marriage should not be for money, but a man should strive to seek a wife who is mild-tempered, tactful, modest and industrious' proliferate in rabbinic literature; and romantic love was not particularly encouraged: 'Charm is a delusion, and beauty fleeting; it is the God-fearing woman who is honored.'[6]

Arranged marriages were considered to be normal and advisable in former times. However, Judaism spurned the idea of an arranged marriage which did not give the young couple time enough to get to know each other before the event and to enter into the marriage of their own free will.

However practical, cautious and even dull this weight of opinion appears, the concept of romantic love also existed; and the first book of the Bible relates how 'Jacob worked seven years for Rachel, and they seemed like a few days because he loved her',[7] and that after being tricked into marrying Leah, he gladly worked for another seven years in

order to become united finally to his beloved Rachel.
Although it is often interpreted allegorically as the relationship
between God and Israel, the Song of Songs must be one of
the most passionate love songs ever written in any language:

> I am my beloved's, his longing is for me.
> Come my beloved, let us go out into the fields
> . . . there will I give you my love. . . .
>
> . . . love is strong as death,
> passion cruel as the grave;
> it blazes up like blazing fire,
> fiercer than any flame.
> Many waters cannot quench love,
> no flood can sweep it away. . . .[8]

In one Talmudic passage the making of a true marriage is
compared in difficulty to the act of parting the Red Sea. No
doubt the practical advice of the Rabbis, the ideals of romantic
love and contemporary ideas on sexual compatibility all have
a part to play in the making of harmonious marriages, blessed
by God.

PREPARATION FOR MARRIAGE

In some western countries, the secular (civil) wedding and
the Jewish (religious) wedding are entirely separate events,
each unrelated to the other. In the United States, ordained
ministers of religion are authorized by the county or state to
solemnize an approved wedding; both the civil and religious
formalities can be completed together. Due notice must be
given to the County Clerk or to City Hall, and any required
blood tests should be taken before a marriage licence is issued.

A similar situation prevails in England, where it is usually
the Secretary of the synagogue who is empowered by the
state to complete the civil formalities.

Various religious considerations will also apply in choosing
a date for the wedding. For traditional couples the date must
be fixed to enable the bride to use the MIKVEH (ritual bath)

before the wedding (see 'Sex in Marriage'). Marriages are not permitted on Sabbaths, festivals, fasts, or on other days of semi-mourning, such as the three weeks preceding the fast of Ab (which commemorates the destruction of the Temple).

The Sabbath before the wedding is the one most often chosen by both families to commence their celebrations. They usually attend synagogue, where the bridegroom is called to the reading of the Torah.

Although most weddings take place in a synagogue, this is merely a matter of convenience and of personal preference. Wedding ceremonies may be carried out at home, in reception halls, in gardens or in the courtyard of the synagogue. All that is needed is a wedding canopy (CHUPPAH), which can be erected anywhere.

The ancient tradition of holding weddings under the open sky is increasingly favored by the more orthodox; the roofs of many synagogue reception halls now include a section that can be opened over the chuppah for this purpose.

Some young couples observe the custom of fasting on the day of their wedding, until after the conclusion of the ceremony, in order to seek spiritual renewal (as on the Day of Atonement) before starting married life together. Bride and bridegroom often refrain from seeing each other for a day before the ceremony, in order to heighten the joy of their meeting under the wedding canopy.

The bride will generally wear white, though this is not essential. She should choose a wedding dress with long sleeves, that covers all parts of her body in keeping with traditional views on modesty of attire. Her hands should be free from rings for the ceremony.

The wedding ring itself must be the property of the bridegroom. It should be an unbroken ring of precious metal, as plain as possible, and must not contain any jewels.

The wedding canopy under which the ceremony takes place symbolizes the marital home. It is a flimsy portable structure – suggesting that the future happiness of the couple will be largely independent of material factors. Indeed a simple TALLIT (prayer shawl), roughly attached to four poles often serves for the Chuppah at marriages held in the open air.

MARRIAGE CONTRACT

In past ages when a woman could be divorced by her husband at will, the provisions of the KETUBAH (marriage contract) were her main financial protection against that eventuality: they also provided for her maintenance after the death of the husband. The marriage settlement specified in the Ketubah was claimable by the wife in case of divorce, and became the first charge on the husband's estate after death. The sum consists of a minimum amount of two hundred ZUZIM for a virgin (the minimum amount for a widow or divorcee is one hundred zuzim), plus a further amount usually negotiated between the bridegroom and the bride's family. (The popular Seder chant indicates the cost of a 'kid' as two zuzim.) These days, when secular civil courts will usually provide women with far greater financial protection than that afforded by the Ketubah, this part of the marriage contract has a significance that is more symbolic than real, even though it remains fully enforceable in law.

The other provisions of the Ketubah concern the husband's obligations to work for, honor, support, clothe, and maintain his wife fully in accordance with established Jewish custom, and to provide her with a full and regular sex life.

The language of the Ketubah is Aramaic. It is sometimes handwritten on parchment; and many beautifully illuminated specimens exist. The document is signed by the bridegroom in the presence of two witnesses; and is then handed to the bride, who retains it as her personal property. In some synagogues the bride will also sign the Ketubah.

A free rendering into English of a modern Sephardi Ketubah is as follows:

On the...day of the...month in the year...since the creation of the world, as we calculate it here in New York on the Hudson River:

Mr . . . said to Miss . . . 'Become my wife according to the law of Moses and Israel. And I, with God's help, will work for, honour, maintain, clothe and support you fully in accordance with Jewish custom. I hereby settle on you the two hundred zuzim that is due to a virgin, and this now belongs to you in accordance with the law of Moses and Israel. I will live with you as a husband according to universal custom, and will undertake all the duties of a faithful husband towards you.'

The bride has consented to become his wife.

The bridegroom has willingly agreed to increase the amount of the settlement by $____. The bridegroom further said:

'I accept for myself and for my heirs full responsibility for the obligation to pay this settlement. It is an obligation in law, and is made without any reservation whatsoever.'

We the undersigned witnesses have taken from the bridegroom, for the benefit of the bride, a solemn pledge, coupled with an oath in the name of the Almighty, that he will carry out all that is written in this Marriage Contract.

Signed: .... (Bridegroom)
Witnessed by: ....
....

MARRIAGE CEREMONY

This consists of two distinct and separate parts. The first ceremony, that of ERUSIN (betrothal) – or KIDDUSHIN (sanctification) – establishes the legal bond between husband and wife: betrothal is roughly equivalent to a modern engagement, with the important difference that a divorce is necessary to break the bond. After the betrothal the couple are legally married, though they are not permitted to live together.

The second ceremony is that of NISSUIN (nuptials), and is celebrated under the Chuppah (wedding canopy). After the nuptials, the marriage is complete and may be consummated.

In Talmudic times there was an interval of at least a year between the two ceremonies, during which the bride remained in her father's house and could not co-habit with the bridegroom. Since the twelfth century the general practice has been to combine the bethrothal and the nuptials as two parts of the same wedding ceremony; though the ancient custom of complete separation still prevails in some remote Sephardi communities.

The order of the modern wedding ceremony varies slightly

between Ashkenazim and Sephardim, and in different communities: however the differences are unimportant and are not fully detailed here.

The service might commence with the reading of the afternoon service, if the timing is suitable: otherwise a selection of psalms may be recited or sung.

The bridegroom and the bride's father, together with two witnesses (often the officiating ministers) will go to the reading desk. The Ketubah (marriage contract), or an extract from it, is read to the bridegroom, who will sign the document and give the traditional pledge to the witnesses as a sign of having taken an oath. The witnesses will then sign the Ketubah.

The bridegroom next proceeds to the Chuppah (marriage canopy) to await the bride. The bride's father escorts the bride into the synagogue and to the canopy, while the choir or cantor sings Psalm 118: 'Blessed be you who comes in the name of the Lord...'

In some communities the bridegroom is escorted by his father and future father-in-law, and the bride by her mother and future mother-in-law. With the bride and groom standing under the canopy together with the officiating minister and both sets of parents, the first part of the ceremony, Erusin (betrothal), begins.

In Ashkenazi synagogues the bride and groom are blessed with the words:

He who is mighty and great above all beings, may He bless the bridegroom and the bride.

The blessings of betrothal are then pronounced over a goblet of wine, and God is praised for having instituted the laws of morality and marriage. The couple then drink the wine, and the bridegroom places the wedding ring on the right index finger of the bride, stating: 'Behold, you are wedded to me by this ring according to the law of Moses and Israel.'

The recital of this formula by the bridegroom, and the willing acceptance of the ring by the bride in the presence of the witnesses, effects the marriage. With this act the ceremony of Erusin is completed.

In some communities the Ketubah (marriage contract), or an extract from it, is read out in English at this stage. Sometimes the Rabbi will deliver the address here: another practice is for the address to be given before the recital of the betrothal blessing.

The Rabbi will then proceed to recite the seven blessings of Nissuin (nuptials) over another goblet of wine:

Blessed are You, O Lord our God, King of the universe, who has created the fruit of the vine.

Blessed are You, O Lord our God, King of the universe, the Creator of man.

Blessed are You, O Lord our God, King of the universe, who has created man in your image . . .

May Zion, who was barren, rejoice at the speedy regathering of her children within her . . .

May this loving couple delight in the same joy that You created at the Garden of Eden. Blessed are You, O Lord, who brings joy to the Bridegroom and to the Bride. Blessed are You, O Lord our God, King of the universe, who has created joy and gladness, Bridegroom and Bride, love and harmony, delight and pleasure, peace and companionship. O Lord our God, may there soon be heard in the cities of Judah and in the streets of Jerusalem the voice of joy and the voice of gladness, the voice of the Bridegroom and the voice of the Bride, the sound of wedding celebrations and the festive songs of youths. Blessed are You, O Lord, who causes the Bridegroom to rejoice with the Bride, and who blesses their welfare. 'Give thanks to the Lord for He is good; for His mercy endures for ever.'

May all sorrows depart from Israel, and may joy increase amongst us.[9]

The bride and groom then drink the wine; and the nuptials are concluded by the bridegroom's breaking a glass (by stamping his foot upon it) as a reminder of the destruction of the Temple – for the Rabbis teach that there must be an element of sorrow, even at moments of the greatest joy. This ends the religious marriage ceremony.

The civil marriage certificate is signed and witnessed

shortly afterwards, usually before the reception. The custom is different in England, where the marriage register is signed by bride, groom and witnesses, who all proceed directly to the reading desk for this purpose before leaving the synagogue.

After the wedding the couple may retire to a room adjoining the synagogue for a few moments of privacy, symbolizing their new status of man and wife, and where they may also break their fast.

The seven nuptial blessings will be recited again after the meal given at the wedding reception; and also (in the presence of the bride and groom) after all meals taken during the first week of marriage, providing that at least ten men are present.

SEX IN MARRIAGE

Judaism regards sex as a normal and essential ingredient of life. It has nevertheless developed detailed laws to channel sexual activity. Put at their very simplest the laws contain two main requirements:

1. Sex is not permitted outside marriage.

2. In marriage, sexual relations may not take place within a woman's menstrual period, or during the week after its end – meaning that sex is barred for at least twelve days in each month.

The Mikveh (ritual bath) is a large bath of specified dimensions. It contains natural spring or rain water; or else may be filled with ordinary tap water and then connected to a source of natural water, such as a rainwater cistern on the roof. A woman is rendered 'ritually impure' by her menstrual flow; and immersion in a Mikveh is required to purify her after menstruation, before she is free to resume sexual relations with her husband. The observant Jewish woman will therefore visit the ritual bath before her marriage, and thereafter every month, one week after the ending of her period.

It must be admitted at once that laws concerning ritual purity and sexual abstinence may seem strange and even archaic to some modern minds. The Rabbis have advanced many different reasons for them, including the idea that they are intended to teach man self-discipline so that he may raise his behaviour above that of the animal world. It is hard to find rational reasons for many of the laws themselves. The ritual bath is not connected with personal hygiene – in fact since earliest times women were required to cleanse themselves before immersion in the Mikveh; and these days they have an ordinary bath first. The notion that physical illness is more likely to afflict those who have sexual relations during the menstrual period is unproven. And the view that twelve consecutive days of abstinence each month serves to enhance mutual pleasure and fertility may or may not be relevant. Much of interest has been written by anthropologists on ancient blood taboos; and the concept of ritual purification by means of immersion is undoubtedly very deep-seated in human consciousness – compare the Hindu practice of bathing in sacred rivers, for example.

However, for the traditional Jew all explanations are unnecessary, interesting though they may be. The laws were given by God to the Jewish people to live by: 'You shall be holy, for I the Lord your God am holy.'[10] Jews are encouraged to discuss their laws and to study them: ultimately, though, the laws exist to be accepted and obeyed. Man will never understand God's purposes and ways: attempts to find satisfying rational explanations for his commandments are secondary, and in most cases futile.

It should be noted that these laws, like many others in the Torah, are intended to apply to Jews only, and to no one else:

> You shall be unto Me a Kingdom of priests, and a holy nation.[11]

PROCREATION AND CONTRACEPTION

Although Judaism recognizes that there are many aspects to a marriage, it expresses little doubt that the procreation of children is a primary purpose. The first commandment that God gave to Adam was: 'Be fruitful and multiply.'[12]

The Rabbis of the Talmudic era differed between themselves to some extent as to just how far a couple must go in order to fulfil the above commandment. The view finally adopted in the HALACHAH (Jewish law) was that put forward by the saintly Hillel at the end of the first century B.C.E., to the effect that the duty to procreate was satisfied after the birth of one male child and one female child.

Answers to questions concerning contraception are not nearly so clear-cut. Apart from the positive command to be fruitful and multiply, the only other direct reference to this subject in the Torah is the description of how Onan was punished by God because he had 'spilled his seed on the ground' to frustrate the purpose of his (levirate) marriage to the childless widow of his elder brother. The question as to whether, and in what circumstances, contraception is allowed is one that must therefore be decided by the Rabbis in each individual case. Quite naturally, one rabbi may differ from another in the interpretation of the law; and some will be more lenient than others. The subject is too technical to be discussed in depth here; and present-day rabbinic opinion can be summarized briefly as follows.

In general, the Rabbis discourage marriage between couples of child-bearing age if procreation is not one of its basic purposes. If both partners are in good health the Rabbis see no good reason to use contraception merely to delay the birth of children. After fulfilling the commandment to be fruitful and multiply, that is, after the birth of a boy and a girl, some rabbis (but not all) may condone the use of contraception in order to space out the birth of further children.

In the case of serious risk to a woman's health, or to that of a future child, the Rabbis would take a very much more lenient view; and some would even require the use of birth control. Psychological (but not social) stresses may be taken into account, as well as risks to physical health. A more permissive view is always taken after the birth of a boy and a girl.

Unlike the Catholic Church, the Jewish religion never suggests abstention from sexual intercourse as a solution to problems that may arise: abstinence is regarded as abnormal and contrary to the very concept of marriage. Jewish law does not permit the male to take birth-control measures (though, even here, one of the leading modern rabbinic scholars disagrees): it is the female who must use the contraceptive, and non-mechanical (e.g. oral) measures are the ones more usually preferred.

As will be realized, Judaism has no rigid rules in these matters; and has no central legislating authority – which may even be one of its strengths. What Divine law (the Torah) does not make clear is left to the Rabbis to interpret; and though such interpretations will always be based on the same fundamental principles, they may possibly change in emphasis from time to time, to suit the needs of the people concerned and the age in which they happen to be living.

ABORTION

In Jewish law the foetus is not regarded as having the same status as a living human being until the larger part of it has emerged from the mother's body. For the first forty days after conception, before the foetus is fully and completely formed, it has almost no status at all. Consequently, though Judaism in general forbids abortion, there are many circumstances in which rabbis are prepared to sanction – and even to require – its practice.

At one extreme, where the mother's life is endangered by the pregnancy there is a positive duty to perform an abortion. On the other hand, abortion for merely social reasons, even during the first forty days, would not be sanctioned.

Health reasons (including psychological ones) which do not endanger the life of the mother fall between the two extremes, as do cases of rape, and cases where there is a probability of the birth of a malformed child. Here rabbis interpret the requirements of the law with a fair amount of elasticity, judging each case on its merits. Some rabbis will take a more tolerant view than others; and all will agree that much more leniency can be allowed during the first forty days after conception, before the foetus is fully formed.

DIVORCE

Divorce is sanctioned and supervised by a Beth Din (rabbinical court) consisting of three judges (rabbis). In Israel, when only Jewish law is used to determine matters of personal status, the Beth Din will also concern itself with a possible reconciliation of the couple, and with matters of maintenance. In English-speaking countries where Jews are subject to the civil law of the land in which they live, no Beth Din will agree to a Jewish divorce until a civil divorce has already been granted in accordance with the laws of the land; and in the overwhelming majority of cases the breach is already final by that stage, with financial and other arrangements completed.

A Jewish divorce is a ceremony in which the biblical injunction that 'He (the husband) writes out for her (the wife) a bill of divorce' is carried out as literally as possible. This bill of divorce is commonly known today as a Get, a word used in the Talmud to describe a legal document. The wording of the Get is very precise, as is the manner of describing the names of the parties in the document. The procedure for writing the bill is complex; and a mistake in a single letter can invalidate the process. Two reasons are advanced for this: the first is that any delay might assist in a possible reconciliation; and the second is based on the importance of the divorce to the woman – after a divorce she is free to remarry at will; but without a valid divorce, sexual relations with another man are adulterous, and were punishable by death in ancient days. The essential wording of the Get is roughly as follows:

I . . ., being under no constraint, do willingly agree to release my wife. . . . Thus do I set free and release you . . . to go and marry any man you may desire. . . . This shall be for you, from me, a bill of divorce . . . in accordance with the law of Moses and Israel.'

The divorce ceremony consists of the man 'writing' a bill of divorce for his wife of his own free will, and of her accepting the document from him of her own free will.

The couple will appear before a Beth Din. One of the judges will give detailed instructions to the husband as to how, precisely, he should prepare the Get. Since the husband will only very rarely possess the expertise with which to write so technical a document (the Get is handwritten, largely in Aramaic), he will in the presence of the court authorize a SOFER (scribe) to write it for him.

The couple will retire whilst the scribe writes the document; and will then return, when the completed Get is meticulously scrutinised by the Beth Din, and signed by two witnesses (who are not members of the court). In a brief formal ceremony, the husband drops the Get into the wife's hands: she walks with it for a few paces to demonstrate that the bill of divorce is now in her possession, and that the divorce is effective. The document is then torn across, to ensure that it cannot be used again.

Divorce is an automatic procedure, providing that it is done with the consent of the husband and of the wife: no reasons are needed, and no matrimonial offences are required as a pretext. However, difficulties can and do arise when only one party agrees to the divorce and the other party resists, as described earlier in this chapter.

Reform synagogues in the United States have a different procedure for dissolving Jewish (religious) marriages, called a Ritual of Release. This takes place before witnesses in the temple, and relies exclusively on the civil divorce certificate. No Get is issued; and the Rabbi always emphasizes that the document given after the ceremony is not a halachic Get (that is, not in accordance with traditional Jewish law). In England, a Get is still the essential ingredient for a divorce undertaken under the auspices of the Reform Movement. In certain circumstances the Reform Beth Din will issue the Get at the wife's request alone, if the husband is unwilling.

4

Death and Mourning

Man goes to his everlasting home, and mourners go about the streets.[1]

THE SYSTEM

The practices and customs of traditional Jews relating to death differ markedly from those of their gentile neighbours. A comprehensive pattern of ritual and behaviour has been developed by the Rabbis throughout the ages in an attempt to cope with almost every possible situation, and very little is left to chance. The Jew is spared the embarrassment and uncertainty so often encountered outside his own circle, of not knowing exactly what to do or to say when faced with a death in the family, or when confronted with the bereaved.

Some may criticize the rigidity and formality of the prescribed observances on the grounds that they leave little room for spontaneous grief, and that mourners should be left on their own at such times, untroubled by the requirements of ancient custom. Against that viewpoint it can be asserted that the Jewish way represents the distillation of many centuries of concern for the bereaved: it recognizes the place for natural feelings of sorrow and anguish, and for their expression; but also, teaching true submission to the will of God, it discourages wild and extravagant displays of emotion. The Rabbis have recognized that close relatives of a recently deceased person are at their most vulnerable, and can easily be upset by a thoughtless word or deed: they have attempted to create a system within which respect for the dead, tender care for the living and acknowledgment of the Divine decree are subtly combined with varying degrees of emphasis during the successive stages which lead from the first moments of grief, through the designated periods of mourning, back to everyday life.

> To everything there is a season, and a time to every purpose under the heaven:
> A time to be born and a time to die . . .
> A time to weep and a time to laugh;
> A time to mourn, and a time to dance. . . .[2]

The path through the valley of the shadow of death is a hard one to tread; but those who are able to lean on the tradition of their fathers can derive a measure of comfort from what is said and done. At the very least they are relieved from the necessity of having to take initiatives and make decisions during the initial numbness of sorrow, and can simply allow themselves to be carried along. Suffering and its disciplines are often found to be curiously enriching experiences in retrospect, helping to deepen sensitivity to the feelings and needs of others.

CARE OF THE DYING

The Jewish faith is far from being fatalistic. A sick person must be nursed with care, and every effort made to preserve the precious gift of life. Indeed, so important is this task that the Rabbis have ruled that even the Sabbath may be broken for that purpose – as the preservation of life takes precedence over almost every other consideration. All the skills of medical science are to be employed; and God's help should also be invoked in private prayer. If requested a special prayer can be recited before the open Ark in a synagogue, the words of which include the following:

> . . . May God who sits on the throne of mercy . . . who answers those who fear Him in time of distress . . . may He regard with compassion, deliver, shield, save, protect and heal (name), who now lies in trouble a... affliction on a bed of sickness . . .

May the supreme King of Kings, through His mercy, heal him (her) with a perfect cure. . . .[3]

However, when the end finally approaches, Jewish teaching is to accept it with resignation and humility as the will of God. Such times can prompt some of the most painful questions that are ever asked – what, for example, can be the Divine purpose in the death of a child, or in that of a truly good person in the prime of life? Why must we suffer? The answer to these questions involves the sum total of human wisdom, with which this brief guide cannot attempt to deal in depth. Perhaps, if a simple answer must be included here, the one given to Job may serve as well as any other. Job, described as a blameless and upright man, answers with perfect resignation when brought news of the loss of all his earthly possessions, and the deaths of his sons and daughters:

> Naked I came from the womb, naked I shall return whence I came. The Lord gave, and the Lord has taken away; blessed be the name of the Lord.[4]

After further terrible afflictions Job was driven to curse the day of his birth: 'Let the day perish wherein I was born.'[5] Unshaken in his integrity, however, Job refuses the temptation to curse God and die. Finally, though, he is driven to question God and to ask why it is that the innocent are made to suffer when the wicked flourish. It is only then that Job is answered, as the Bible so poetically puts it, from the depths of a whirlwind. 'Who is this,' asks God majestically, 'whose ignorant words cloud my design in darkness?'

> Where were you when I laid the earth's foundations?
> Tell me if you know and understand . . .
> In all your life have you ever called up the dawn, or shown the morning its place? . . .
> Have you descended to the springs of the sea or walked in the unfathomable deep? . . .
> Have you comprehended that vast expanse of the world? . . .[6]

In other words, man's powers of comprehension are puny:

he can never aspire to understand in any real sense the ways or purposes of the Divine: he can only accept his lot, secure in the belief of a higher form of existence than his own, and in 'the world to come'.

In so far as the actual process of dying is concerned, the Jewish way is simply that of kindness, consideration and common sense. There are no special procedures: all that is required is to ease the passage of the dying, and to spare the feelings of the grieving family as far as possible. The dying person must not be left alone, and must not be shocked or frightened in any way.

Where appropriate a general prayer and confession is recited, the text of which will be found in most prayer books, and which includes the following phrases:

Lord of the universe, Lord of forgiveness and mercy . . . I acknowledge before You that both my cure and my death are in Your hands: may it be Your will to heal me with a perfect cure . . . but if the time appointed for me be near, let my death be an atonement for all my sins and transgressions. . . . Let my portion be in Paradise, and grant me that world to come which is treasured up for the righteous . . .
Into Your hand I commit my spirit . . .
Hear O Israel, the Lord is our God, the Lord is one.[7]

Even so, many authorities recommend that such prayer should not be urged on a sick person if there is any risk of causing distress, and thereby of shortening life.

When death does come, the son or nearest kin will reverently close the eyes and mouth, the arms and hands will be extended at each side of the body, the face and body will be covered by a plain white sheet, and a candle or other light will be left burning close by the head. After the first shock has lessened, someone should contact the local synagogue, funeral home or burial society, from which further advice will be forthcoming.

ARRANGEMENTS FOR BURIAL

Jewish law requires that burial shall take place as soon as possible after death, which practice conflicts sharply with that of Christian society. There may even be a feeling that it is unseemly and unfeeling to shuffle the deceased out of sight so quickly. On the contrary, the tradition of early burial has as its primary purpose the wish to show respect to the dead; for in Jewish, as in other ancient cultures, the unburied state is regarded as, in some way, humiliating. Nevertheless burial must be delayed (though most reluctantly) if specifically ordered by the secular authorities for a post-mortem examination; and the rabbi himself may permit a short voluntary delay, mainly in order to await the arrival of a principal mourner.

Before the funeral takes place the bereaved family is in a transitional stage: the period of formal mourning has not commenced, yet life cannot continue as usual. Statutory daily prayers are not recited, Tefillin are not worn, normal work is not permitted, meat and wine are not consumed, sexual activity ceases. The only task allowed to the ONEN – for that is what the mourner is called before the burial – is caring for the dead by making arrangements for the funeral, attending the body and preparing it for burial.

The first duty is to obtain a death certificate from the doctor in attendance. A doctor not acquainted with Jewish custom will be unaware of the need for haste, and may well leave the house without completing the death certificate unless reminded to do so.

In the United States, most funerals are arranged through a funeral home to which the corpse is taken as soon as possible after death. The funeral director will arrange for compliance with the various civil requirements once the death certificate has been issued. The rites of purification (Tahara) are carried out at the funeral home, and the funeral service takes place in its chapel. If a funeral home is not used, Tahara may take place at the home of the deceased and the funeral service may take place there or sometimes even at the cemetery itself.

In England, where most funerals are arranged through burial societies attached to synagogues, the death certificate must be taken personally by the next of kin to the Registrar for Births and Deaths, without whose release certificate no burial can lawfully take place. This formality, tiresome during a period of great distress, has to be attended to promptly in order to avoid delay. Trouble arises when the Registrar's office is closed, or else too busy to deal with the release certification at once. At the same time, the appropriate Jewish burial society will have to be contacted and arrangements made for the funeral. The entire funeral service usually takes place in a special 'prayer hall' adjacent to the cemetery.

It is important to inform relatives and friends of the funeral arrangements at the earliest possible opportunity, for there is usually very little time available.

Meanwhile the corpse, in keeping with proper feelings of respect, may not be left unattended. This will be much easier to carry out if death takes place at home, where the watchers will usually read from the Psalms or Lamentations.

In Ashkenazi homes mirrors are covered or else turned inwards to the wall. Many reasons are given for this, ranging from the frankly superstitious to the more rational – such as the avoidance of symbols of vanity. Sephardim do not generally have this custom.

Those charged by the Jewish community with the rites of TAHARA (purification) are religiously observant Jews. They are known in most Ashkenazi communities as the HEVRA KADISHA (holy brotherhood or sisterhood) and in Sephardi communities as LAVADORES (or Lavadoras). Though the members are often paid officials, many communities pride themselves on providing these last offices on a voluntary basis. In such congregations the society or brotherhood will include some of the most distinguished men and women of the community, who remain available to be called from their homes or places of work at short notice in order to perform this sacred duty. The service is performed anonymously; and as it is for the dead alone, no thanks for it can ever be expressed in this world.

The actual purification is either carried out at home, at the funeral home or (in England) in a special room adjoining the cemetery. If at home, everything other than water for the washing is brought to the house. The rites consist of reverently washing and drying the body, dressing it in plain white shrouds, and placing it in the coffin. Men are also dressed in a Tallit (prayer shawl); and in some communities a small amount of TERRA SANTA (soil from the Holy Land) is also placed in the coffin.

Though Jewish law requires the body to be buried in its

shrouds alone, this is not permitted in western countries, where the use of a coffin is obligatory. Traditional Jewish coffins are made from plain unpolished wooden boards, and no adornment whatsoever is allowed: in death, all are equal.

Non-orthodox practices differ from the traditional, sometimes quite considerably. The rites of purification (Tahara) are rarely carried out on those belonging to the Conservative movement, and do not form a part of the Reform ritual. The corpse may be clad in shrouds, but is more usually dressed in ordinary clothes. Elaborate caskets, sometimes of metal, are used, and there is often an open-coffin viewing of the deceased by relatives and friends. Flowers are prominently displayed at such funerals.

Some mention must be made at this stage of the actual custom of burial, which has been the Jewish method of dealing with the dead since earliest times. Burning and embalming were regarded as pagan rites and are prohibited by Jewish law. The Jewish view is eloquently stated in Ecclesiastes:

> Then shall the dust return to the earth as it was; and the spirit shall return unto God who gave it.[8]

The human body, dwelling place of the soul, and part of the highest form of creation must always be treated with reverence:

> God created man in His own image . . . male and female He created them.[9]

The Rabbis regard the reduction of a corpse to ashes by fire as an indignity and an outrage. Consequently, no traditional Jewish organization will sanction cremation. If cremation has already taken place, some traditional Jewish burial societies may agree to bury the ashes in an ordinary coffin in the normal manner. Others will refuse to do so.

Reform temples and most conservative and progressive synagogues allow cremation, and will provide a normal funeral service to accompany it.

RENDING OF GARMENTS

KERIAH (rending) is the traditional Jewish sign of grief, first mentioned early in the Book of Genesis, when Jacob was brought the mangled and blood-stained coat of Joseph:

> Jacob rent his clothes, put on sackcloth, and mourned his son. . . .[10]

The rite is performed at home, on hearing of the death of one's parent, spouse, child, brother or sister. It may also be carried out at the cemetery.

The mourner stands; and a vertical tear (started by a cut) is made down the jacket, shirt or under-garment. This is done on the left hand side for the death of a parent, and on the right hand side in other cases. The following blessing is recited: 'Blessed are You O Lord our God, King of the universe, the true Judge.'

For a parent, the rent must never be fully mended, though it may be stitched together roughly after thirty days. For other relatives it may be repaired loosely after seven days, and the repair completed after thirty days.

Non-traditional rabbis will often provide mourners with a pin-on ribbon to be torn.

FUNERAL SERVICE AND BURIAL

The funeral may well provide mourners with one of their saddest and most moving experiences. It will be hard for them to derive much comfort from the proceedings, which are designed to engender a mood of acceptance and finality. Expressions of grief are considered normal, and are not suppressed by non-assimilated Jews. Others, less closely involved, will perhaps be impressed by the simple dignity of the ceremony, and by the kindness and sympathy of those present.

Flowers are strongly discouraged at traditional Jewish burials. It may save embarrassment at a sensitive time if non-

orthodox Jews and non-Jewish friends can be warned tact-
fully not to send flowers or wreaths.

In many communities women did not attend funerals until
comparatively recently, but simply remained at home or in
the house of mourning. These days most women do go to
funerals, and some to the actual burial. In more orthodox
communities, women may still be asked to stand away from
the graveside during the interment.

The funeral service is simple. The coffin is brought into the
funeral chapel, and the memorial address (if any) is delivered. The short service can be lengthened to an hour or so if
relatives and friends deliver eulogies. Psalms and appropriate
verses from the Bible are read, and, in the Sephardi ritual,
some present make seven circuits round the bier (of a male),
while chanting prayers for the soul of the deceased:

> Have mercy upon him, we beseech you . . . and may his
>   soul be held in the bond of life. . . .
> Remember the good that he did in life. . . .
> May the Gracious One, in the abundance of His mercy,
>   forgive his transgressions. . . .
> May he find the gates of Heaven open . . . and may the
>   angels receive him there. . . .
> May his soul go to the cave of Machpelah . . . may it be
>   admitted to Paradise. . . .
> May Michael open the gates of the sanctuary, and bring his
>   soul as an offering before God. . . .
> May his soul be bound up in the bond of life . . . and may
>   he walk forever in the land of life. . . .[11]

Ashkenazim actually start the service with a passage
acknowledging the justice of God's decree, while Sephardim
say this after the burial:

> You are righteous, O Lord; and true are your judgments.
> The Lord is just in all His ways, and merciful in all His
> works. . . . The Rock, His work is perfect for all His ways
> are just. . . .

When the service has been held in a funeral home, the coffin is then taken by motorcade to the cemetery for burial, or else to the airport if the body is to be interred elsewhere. When, as in England, the service is held in a prayer hall adjoining the cemetery, the coffin is simply carried into the cemetery. More rarely, the entire service may be conducted at the graveside.

The coffin is carried to the grave, sometimes by pallbearers, and is followed by the mourners, relatives and friends. The ancient custom, when still observed, of halting several times on the way in order to recite passages from Psalm 91, adds considerably to the poignancy of the occasion.

As the coffin is being lowered into the grave, Ashkenazim say: 'May he come to his place in peace.' Sephardim read Psalm 91:

. . . The Lord is my refuge and my fortress . . . He will cover you with His wings, and you shall find safety beneath them . . . He has charged His angels to guard over you, wherever you may go. . . .

Afterwards the grave is filled with earth by those present, each in turn placing three spadefuls of soil on the coffin (symbolising the three parts of the soul). The spade is not passed from hand to hand, but is returned to the ground by each person, and taken up again by the next in line.

In non-orthodox burials, the coffin is not always covered with earth by the mourners and friends, but may just be covered temporarily with a cloth, and buried later.

The burial service concludes with the recitation of a psalm, with the memorial prayer for the soul of the departed, and with the recitation of Kaddish by the male mourners. A general memorial prayer is sometimes added for all those buried in the cemetery.

On leaving the cemetery, all wash their hands with water (the symbol of life) and say:

"He will destroy death for ever; and the Lord God will wipe away tears from every face; and will remove all insult to His people from the earth – for the Lord has spoken it".

Sometimes the following verse from Deuteronomy is recited:
Our hands have not shed this blood, neither have our eyes
seen it.

The burial service follows generally along the broad lines
indicated above. Details of the ceremony and its precise order
vary from place to place and from time to time, in accordance with local custom, with the calendar, and with the
time of day.

When the proceedings are over, it is usual for those present to greet the mourners, murmuring words of sympathy
and consolation. In the Sephardi tradition it is usual to shake
hands. In England it has become customary to wish mourners
"long life".

MEMORIAL PRAYER

The memorial prayer, said after the burial, is also recited at
services held in the house of mourning during the following
week. In Sephardi synagogues the identical prayer is read
aloud on all those occasions when the dead are remembered,
as well as on the Day of Atonement. In Ashkenazi synagogues
the memorial prayer, in a slightly different form – known as
YISKOR (may God remember) – is recited on Passover,
Shavuot, Shemini Azeret, and on the Day of Atonement.

The Ashkenazi version, EL MALE RAHAMIM (God, full of
compassion), usually sung by the cantor with high emotion,
seldom fails to bring tears to the eyes of at least some of its
hearers. The Sephardi prayer, known as HASHKABAH (laying
to rest), is simply recited and has less immediate impact.

As this is the only prayer which specifically mentions the
deceased by name, the whole service can be rendered more
meaningful for those with little Hebrew if the memorial prayer
can be repeated in English. This is often done, at least in
part; but the Reader should be reminded, if that is the
mourners' wish.

Free renderings into English of different versions of the
memorial prayer are as follows.

An Ashkenazi version:

O Lord and King who is full of compassion, God of all
flesh, in whose hands are the souls of the living and the
dead, receive we beseech you, in your great loving kindness,

the soul of (*name*), who has been gathered to his (her) people.

Have mercy upon him (her) and pardon his (her) transgressions; for there is none so righteous on earth that he does only good, and sins not. Remember his good deeds in his favour, and bring him to his reward.

Shelter his soul in the shadow of your wings, and bring him to the path of life. In your presence is fullness of joy, and at your right hand is eternal bliss.

Bestow upon him the great happiness that is stored up for the righteous. As it is written: 'How great is the goodness which You have reserved for them that fear You, which You have made for them that trust entirely in You.'

O Lord who heals the broken-hearted and binds up their wounds, grant consolation to the mourners. Strengthen and support them at their time of sorrow and grief; and remember them and their children for a long and good life. Put the fear and the love of God into them, that they may serve You with a perfect heart; and bring them peace.

As one whom his mother comforts, so will I comfort you (says the Lord); and in Jerusalem shall you be comforted. The sun shall no more go down for you, neither shall the moon wane – for the Lord shall be your everlasting light; and the days of your mourning shall be ended.

The Lord God will wipe away tears from every face, and will remove all insult to His people from the earth – for the Lord has spoken it.

A Sephardi version (Hashkabah):

A good name smells sweeter than precious perfume; and the day of one's death is better than the day of one's birth. In the end, the whole duty of man is to fear God and keep His commandments.

May the pious be joyful in glory, and rejoice in their rest.

May the resting place of the soul of our departed brother (*name*) be under the wings of the Divine Presence, where the holy and pure souls shine resplendent, where virtue is strengthened, trespasses pardoned and sin kept far distant. May salvation, grace and compassion come from Him who is enthroned on high.

May his be a good portion in the world to come; and may the Lord give him rest in Paradise – for he did depart this world according to the will of God, the Lord of heaven and earth.

May the supreme King of kings have pity and compassion on him. May he rest in peace, as it is written: 'The upright shall enter into peace: peace shall be their repose.'

May he, and all Israel who sleep in the grave with him, be included in God's mercy and forgiveness.

May this be the Divine Will; and let us say Amen.

KADDISH

The Kaddish is of ancient origin, and dates from before the destruction of the Temple. The word 'Kaddish' is Aramaic (the everyday language spoken by most Jews of that time) for 'holy'; and the prayer is written in a mixture of Aramaic and Hebrew. It is both an expression of praise and glorification of God, and a messianic prayer calling for the speedy establishment of his kingdom on earth. The Kaddish may only be said in public when at least ten males are present; and is recited standing, and facing towards Jerusalem.

It was originally employed to conclude the regular public expositions of the Torah, which had become an established feature of Jewish life by the end of the first century B.C.E. This was done to demonstrate the belief that study of the Torah is not only an intellectual pursuit, but is also the beginning of knowledge that leads to the love and to the fear of God. The Kaddish is still used, roughly in this manner, to mark the conclusion of certain sections of the synagogue service.

The Kaddish was first adopted by mourners as a prayer specially suited to their needs during the period of severe persecution of Jews in the thirteenth century (the Crusades). It is now the only public prayer recited by mourners.

Though difficult to capture the full flavour of the Kaddish in translation, the following free version of the form most frequently used by mourners will give a fair impression:

MOURNER: Glorified and sanctified be God's great name throughout the world, which He has created according to His will. May He establish His Kingdom (cause salvation to spring forth and hasten the coming of His Messiah – Sephardim only) in your lifetime and within that of the whole House of Israel, speedily and soon.
And let us say Amen.

CONGREGATION: May His great Name be blessed for ever and ever.

MOURNER: May His great Name be blessed for ever and ever. Blessed and praised, glorified and exalted, adored and honoured, be the Name of the Holy One, blessed be He, far more than any blessings and praises that can ever be uttered in this world.
And let us say Amen.
May abundant peace descend from heaven, with life (and plenty, healing and liberation, atonement and forgiveness, redemption and salvation – Sephardim only) for us and for all Israel.
And let us say Amen.
May He who creates perfect harmony in His heavens (through His infinite mercy – Sephardim only) grant peace to us and to all Israel.
And let us say Amen.

When the Kaddish is recited immediately after the reading of a rabbinic passage in the service, the following additional verse is inserted:

For Israel, for our Rabbis, for their disciples and pupils, and for all who study the Torah, here and everywhere – for them and for us, may grace, loving kindness and mercy come from the Lord of heaven and earth.
And let us say Amen.

To those with little understanding of Jewish liturgy, it may appear strange that these particular verses have been chosen above all others as the mourner's prayer; for they contain no reference to death, or to the soul of the departed. Indeed at first sight the Kaddish may seem too impersonal for such use; and it is hard to blame those who, glancing superficially at the text, conclude that this long recitation of Aramaic and Hebrew words is a mere formula, devoid of true relevance.

Man is obliged to praise his Creator at all times; but when he has just lost a loved one, and has the greatest temptation to doubt God, that act of praise has heightened significance. It then expresses resignation to the will of God and submission to his judgment, rather in the spirit of Job's declaration on the loss of his children: 'The Lord has given: the Lord has taken away: blessed be the name of the Lord.'[12] Man's longing for the coming of the messianic age, when God's Kingdom will be established on earth, is at its most intense at times of suffering; and the messianic aspect of the Kaddish therefore becomes specially appropriate at moments of acute personal distress. Viewed in this light the Kaddish is an eloquent declaration of submission to God's decree, coupled with a plea for the early advent of the final redemption, when pain and suffering in the world will cease for ever.

The core of the Kaddish is considered to be the congregation's response to the mourner, 'YEHE SHEME RABBA MEBARACH . . .' (May His great Name be blessed and glorified for ever and ever); and this is the key to a range of further meanings assigned to this ancient prayer. Jewish tradition holds that God rewards us for the good deeds of our parents, and indeed for those of our forefathers. In like manner therefore it is argued that parents can benefit after death from the merit of their children. Consequently the recital of the Kaddish by a mourner becomes particularly significant; for it is hoped that the deceased parent may thus be rewarded for the mourner's pious act of leading the congregation in prayer, and causing those present to bless and glorify God's great Name in their responses.

Of course it will come as no surprise to those acquainted with Kabbalah to learn that the mystics have also derived hidden meanings from the words, and even from the letters comprising the words of the Kaddish. The simplest of these explanations, and the one which has most captured the public's imagination, is again based on the great value attached to the congregation's response 'Yehe Sheme Rabba . . .'. Kabbalists have gone so far as to maintain that the 'evil decree' is cancelled for those who make this response in a spirit of true devotion; and also that 'evil decrees' against the House of Israel as a whole are continually deferred from day to day because of the responses of its people. According to Kabbalah, the souls of the departed are punished for their sins on earth for a period of up to twelve months after death; and the congregation's response in the Kaddish has the power of instantly lessening this suffering. Thus the recital of Kaddish by a son of the deceased is a form of direct intercession for the soul of his parent – in other words, a prayer of special efficacy for the dead, as it is in fact generally regarded. Widespread though this idea became, it was also opposed by some rabbis, who warned that the dead would be judged for their actions on earth, and not on account of the prayers offered by their sons. They preferred to view the Kaddish as a method of honoring the memory of a parent, by causing a congregation to assemble and join the mourner in giving public praise to God.

As a mourner's prayer the Kaddish was at first recited only by sons for their parents during the first eleven months of mourning. (It was considered disrespectful to assume that the soul of the dead parent would require the maximum period of twelve months punishment.) It was later extended in scope; and it is now said for grandparents, by fathers for children, by brothers for sisters, and even for a stranger when there is no one available who is better qualified.

On the whole, women do not say Kaddish (though some rabbis permit them to do so); but simply respond with the rest of the congregation.

Recital of the Kaddish is not intended to be a test of a person's linguistic fluency. The practice of rattling through the prayer at great speed is much to be regretted, as this can detract both from its meaning and from its impact. When read slowly by a mourner, with full concentration and devotion, the Kaddish assumes a sublime dimension; and its recitation becomes a moving experience both for the mourner and for those who listen to him and respond to his lead.

MOURNING

> My son, shed bitter tears for the dead; raise a lament for
> your grievous loss . . . with bitter tears and passionate
> lament, make your mourning worthy. . . .[13]

The concept of the 'stiff upper lip' is not accepted in Judaism,
which has always regarded displays of emotion as natural,
healthy and entirely appropriate to times of great sorrow or
great joy.

Jews are however warned by their sages that mourning
must be restrained both in manner and in duration: 'Mourn
for a while . . . and then take comfort. . . . Do not abandon
yourself to grief. . . . You cannot help him, and can only
injure yourself.'[14]

Tradition recognizes three main periods of formal mourning – the first week, the first month, and the first year. These
are decreed to honor the memory of the dead, and to impose
some limit on the suffering of the mourners. They are also
intended as a discipline, by means of which the mourners
may be led back in stages from the initial numbness of grief
to normal life. The mourning process therefore proceeds in a
set pattern which has changed little in its essentials since
Talmudic times.

SHIVAH

> . . . Joseph observed seven days mourning for his father.[15]

SHIVAH (seven) is observed for a parent, spouse, child, brother
or sister. The period commences with the day of the burial
(day one); and continues for seven days, unless prematurely
terminated by the advent of one of the festivals, the New
Year, or the Day of Atonement. No mourning is permitted
on the Sabbath, a day of joy; so formal mourning is suspended
for that day, even though it is included as one of the seven.
The first three days, described as the time of weeping, is the
strictest period; and mourning may be slightly less intense
during the last four days, known as the time of lamentation.

On returning home from the funeral, mourners eat the

Meal of Consolation. This is served to them by their friends, who provide the food specially and bring it to the house: it consists usually of bread and hard boiled eggs, which symbolise the continuity of life. A memorial candle is lit and the light maintained for the full seven days: candles, each lasting for twenty-four hours, are readily available for this use.

Except for possible visits to the synagogue, mourners are obliged to remain in the house of mourning for the entire week. They no longer sit on the ground, wear sackcloth and sprinkle ashes over their heads as in former days; but now sit on low chairs or stools, refrain from wearing leather shoes and slippers indoors, and dress sombrely and with discretion. The wearing of black is no longer as widespread as it was; and this is now even positively discouraged in some communities.

Other than in exceptional circumstances, mourners may not work or pursue any occupation during the Shivah. Mourners are not allowed to shave, to cut their hair and nails, or to wear cosmetics. All forms of entertainment and pleasurable activity (including sexual relations) are forbidden; and this ban extends even to the reading and study of Torah, other than for certain mournful passages such as Lamentations, the Book of Job, and the laws of mourning.

Statutory daily services are held in the house of mourning every day, except on the Sabbath; though where this is not practicable they may be held in the synagogue. Morning service is usually timed before breakfast. The afternoon service (immediately followed by the evening service) is held in the early part of the evening. The order of service is varied slightly from the usual, with the addition of the memorial prayer and the omission of various passages considered to be inappropriate: mourners recite the Kaddish.

As will be appreciated, the rules of mourning fulfil several main functions, the first of which is to show fitting respect for the memory of the dead. So far as the mourners themselves are concerned, Shivah serves to shield them from the strains and distractions of everyday life at the time of their greatest vulnerability; and to allow a pause within which they can attempt to adjust gradually to their loss. This retreat from the normal world can also provide a rare opportunity for self-examination, and for a fundamental reassessment of the mourner's own life, values and priorities, all in the context of the inescapable fact of death.

Judaism stresses the obligation to comfort mourners; and the attitude and behaviour of friends and neighbours can be of critical importance during the Shivah. Friends will visit the house of mourning frequently, to sit with the mourners: letters and telephone calls are no substitute for this, unless long distances prevent personal contact. Men can help considerably by attending the morning and evening services at the house (or in the synagogue), in order to ensure that Kaddish can be recited – ten men form the necessary quorum; and the gesture of getting up early in the morning to be present at such services is one that is often gratefully remembered long after the event.

Visitors to a house of mourning should always respect the sensitivity of its occupants, who may well be in a highly emotional state. On entering, visitors should sit down unobtrusively and converse quietly: it is customary for them not to greet the mourners first – their duty is to respond when required, and simply to be there in the hope that their presence may be of comfort. Some Sephardim have a different custom; and most will go up to the mourners, shake hands with each in turn and murmur words of sympathy. All too often, when many people are present, conversation can tend to become noisy, and even jolly: such clamor, more appropriate to a celebration than to a house of mourning, can very easily cause great offence. It is clearly impossible to lay down a set pattern of behavior, for people vary so much in their needs and attitudes; but most mourners appreciate gentle and sympathetic conversation, and even some mild distraction. They will usually react badly to obvious attempts to cheer them up (however well-intentioned), preferring to remain close to their sorrow for the short time available. The very presence of a large number of people can be jarring in itself; and visitors should do their best to minimize any disturbance. Tactful friends will space their visits with care; and will leave just as soon as they feel that they are not contributing further to the mourners' comfort. On leaving the house, visitors should approach the mourners, and express the wish that they may be "comforted with the other mourners of

Zion." The substitution of a less formal expression is very much a matter of personal taste and judgment.

Though tea and biscuits, and even cakes, are sometimes served to visitors, there are many who will prefer to serve nothing at all, or to adopt the practice of some communities who offer only cups of black coffee, or tea without milk. Many people, quite understandably, regard the sight of fancy biscuits or cakes as distasteful at such a time.

Well-wishers often bring food to the mourners. This is a very old custom that has as its object the wish to spare the mourners the effort and distraction of having to provide food for themselves. The bringing of a meal, or part of a meal, by neighbors and friends for this purpose is an act of kindness that is usually very much appreciated. Unfortunately the practice, when not properly understood, can go badly wrong – to the extent that the 'food' can become a box of chocolates, even gift-wrapped on occasion. Gifts as such (including chocolates!) must never be brought; and it is both wrong and tactless to do so. Cakes and biscuits are sometimes given; and they may be useful and acceptable when intended for serving to other visitors – though views have already been expressed on the suitability of offering this type of refreshment.

In some communities the rabbi will call at the house of mourning at the conclusion of the Shivah in order to 'raise' the mourners from their state. After reciting a short prayer he will physically help the mourners up from their low stools to mark the ending of the Shivah.

The whole concept of Shivah, with its formal patterns and disciplines, is sometimes questioned and even attacked in these days of spontaneity and free expression. The Rabbis and Sages, who developed its structure throughout the long span of Jewish history, certainly were no fools. Many of them, numbered amongst the wisest and most perceptive of men, were also shrewd judges of human nature – which changes little, despite different manners acquired in different places and at different times. The Shivah is an institution of value, that corresponds to basic human needs. It should not be abbreviated or curtailed, for most people will benefit from its observance – providing, of course, that this is carried out with intelligence, based on adequate knowledge and understanding of its meaning.

SHELOSHIM

> . . . and the children of Israel mourned thirty days for
> Aaron. . . .[16]

SHELOSHIM (thirty) is the name given to the prescribed month
of mourning, starting on the day of the burial (day one), and
continuing for thirty days. This mourning period is observed
for a parent, spouse, child, brother or sister.

After the end of the Shivah (first seven days), the requirements of mourning become very much less onerous, with the
mourners returning to work and to most of their usual
everyday activities.

Mourners are still forbidden to shave or to cut their hair:
they may not marry, or visit places of entertainment:
attending festivities, listening to music and similar pleasurable
activity is not allowed. Mourners are required to attend daily
services at the synagogue, and to recite Kaddish.

Most mourners will be ready to take the first steps towards resuming normal life by the time the Shivah had
ended. The remaining three weeks or so of the Sheloshim is a
useful transition, during which the necessary adjustments can
be made.

YEAR OF MOURNING

For a parent only, mourning continues for a full year from
the day of burial, though in a much modified form.

The only practical restriction that remains after the ending
of Sheloshim is the ban on attending places of entertainment,
or festivities, particularly where music is played. Though not
allowed to shave during the year, the Rabbis permit this rule
to be relaxed as soon as the mourner is 'reproached' by friends
or acquaintances for looking unkempt.

The conscientious male mourner will continue to attend the
daily services in the synagogue, so that he may recite Kaddish
during the first eleven months (see section above on Kaddish).

The periods of one year, and of eleven months, are measured in accordance with the Jewish calendar (see below,
Anniversary).

MEMORIAL STONE

At some time during the first year, and usually towards the end of the period, it is customary to place a tombstone over the grave of the deceased. Ashkenazim generally wait for the full year before erecting the memorial. Rules concerning the inscription vary from community to community; but the text is usually fairly simple, and is inscribed in both Hebrew and English. Ashkenazi tombstones are fixed in a vertical position; and those for Sephardim are laid flat over the grave. Guidance on all practical details can be obtained from the rabbi, or from the local burial authorities.

A service for unveiling or consecrating the memorial stone at the cemetery is usual, although not required by Jewish law. It is attended by mourners, relatives and friends. Psalms are recited, and a memorial address is often delivered. Mourners say Kaddish. The practice of offering refreshment after the ceremony has, regrettably, become widespread. On the whole it is preferable to restrict this to the immediate family and to those who have travelled some distance to attend. Any suggestion of a 'party' should be avoided.

ANNIVERSARY

The anniversary of the death of a parent is known as YAHRZEIT to Ashkenazim, and as NAHALAH (or Annos) to Sephardim: it is marked in a special manner.

The Yahrzeit, or Nahalah, is observed on each anniversary of death according to the Jewish calendar. It must be remembered that as the Jewish and secular calendars do not coincide, the occasion will occur on different dates each year according to the secular calendar. Corresponding dates are obtainable from the *Encyclopaedia Judaica*, or from other reference books: many synagogues will send a special card of reminder every year, on request.

On the Sabbath prior to the anniversary the son of the deceased should ask to be called to the reading of the Torah in the synagogue; and a memorial prayer will be read. Kaddish will be recited.

Most will observe the actual day of the anniversary quietly, refraining from obvious amusement, studying Torah a little, and dispensing charity. Sons will attend the daily services at a synagogue, where they will recite the Kaddish. Some observe the custom of fasting on the day, as a special mark of respect for the dead, and as a sign of personal repentence; and many will light a memorial candle at home, and keep this burning for the full twenty-four hours as a sign of remembrance.

COHEN

A COHEN (priest), as a descendant of Aaron the High Priest, is still subject to the ancient laws concerning the ritual purity of the priesthood.

A Cohen may not therefore be under the same roof (literally) as a corpse. For this reason he will not enter the house of a dying person, in case death should suddenly occur; and at the cemetery he will remain outside the prayer hall while the coffin is within. Likewise a Cohen may not approach close to a grave.

These restrictions do not apply for the Cohen's own parents, wife, children, or brother; they do not apply for the sister of a Cohen, providing that she was unmarried and that they both had the same father.

SUICIDE

Judaism regards human life as being so precious that all the commandments of the Torah – save those relating to idolatry, murder and immorality – may be broken for its preservation. Consequently the taking of one's own life, if consciously premeditated, is a crime against God. According to the strict application of Jewish law therefore, a suicide must be buried quietly in a corner of the cemetery. There is no funeral service, and no formal mourning is allowed.

However, as in many similar matters, the rabbis have and do exercise considerable discretion in the interests of compassion. Other than in the most exceptional cases it is now considered that suicide is more an act of despair, committed when the mind is disturbed (by pain or grief), than a wilful act of defiance of Divine law. Hence most rabbis, giving the benefit of any doubt that may exist, will permit full burial and mourning rites.

EUTHANASIA

Positive acts of euthanasia are totally forbidden, and are equated with murder in Jewish law. Human life is regarded as a precious gift from God, and only God can end life. Man in his ignorance may not interfere with the Divine will by doing anything intended to shorten life – whether it is someone else's life, or one's own.

However a new situation has arisen recently because of the discovery of modern 'miracle' drugs, and the development of life-supporting machines to prolong life artificially, well beyond the stage at which it would naturally have ended. Rabbinical opinion is still developing in these matters; but some kind of consensus is already emerging.

At one end of the range, most rabbis condone not starting on a course of medical treatment, if its only purpose is to extend a lingering life of suffering without hope of recovery. Many rabbis would sanction the withdrawal of life-support equipment in certain circumstances, where this is prolonging life artificially for no good purpose. More controversial is the permissibility of administering large doses of pain-killing drugs, where a known side-effect is to shorten the life of the patient – and here opinions differ sharply.

Though Judaism forbids the committing of positive acts to shorten life, it teaches that there are circumstances in which man is not obliged to prolong life artificially beyond its natural span. Precise definition of these circumstances and the required precautions to be taken are highly complex and not easily decided, even by the rabbi who may be asked for a ruling on a particular case.

Part II

The Framework of Belief

5

Traditional Concepts

REVELATION

Traditional Judaism, as a faith, is firmly based on revelation. In Jewish history God appeared first to the patriarchs – Abraham, Isaac and Jacob – and then to Moses.

In an awesome encounter with the entire nation of Israel gathered together at the foot of Mount Sinai, God revealed himself to each one of them, collectively and individually. That pivotal event – the giving of the Ten Commandments – so impressed itself on the consciousness of the people that a MIDRASH (rabbinic parable) has it that all future generations of Jews, yet unborn, were also present at Sinai for that unique revelation.

Through Moses, described in the Bible as the man of God, the Divine message was transmitted to the Jews in the form of the TORAH ('teaching', though often inadequately translated as 'law') in two parallel parts – the written Torah consisting of the first books of the Bible, the Five Books of Moses (Genesis, Exodus, Leviticus, Numbers and Deuteronomy), and the oral Torah which is that body of traditional teaching faithfully passed on by word of mouth from one generation to the next.

Accounts of God's further revelations to man are contained in the later books of the Bible. But it is the Torah itself that is the foundation of the Jewish religion; and it is belief in its Divine origin that is one of Judaism's most basic dogmas. In the light of received tradition, successive generations of Rabbis have been able to deepen the understanding of the Torah in their own times by successive re-interpretations of its shades of meaning: however the actual words of the written Torah and the principles enshrined therein are regarded as God-given, immutable and eternal.

Moses first encountered God on a journey through the desert, when he paused with amazement beside a bush that continued to burn without being consumed. In answer to Moses's question concerning his identity, God replied:

'I AM; that is who I am',[1]

and that answer illustrates well the traditional attitude to the nature of the Divine, about which mainstream Judaism hardly ever speculates. God is regarded simply as pure spirit – whatever that may mean – an unknown essence, incapable of comprehension by the human mind. Indeed in a well-known Midrash God is represented as saying to his people: 'Would that you would forget ME; but keep my Torah.'[2]

In complete contrast, those qualities by means of which God makes himself known to man are revealed in great detail in the Torah: to Moses, God described himself as:

A God compassionate and gracious, long-suffering and abundant in mercy and truth . . . forgiving iniquity, transgression and sin . . . but one who punishes. . . .[3]

In yet another passage, the Israelites are commanded: 'You shall be holy, for I the Lord your God am holy',[4] and the ritual, moral and ethical constituents of such 'holiness' are closely defined: indeed the duties of ritual observance, of doing justice and of practising righteousness are so interwoven in the ideal of 'holiness' as a way of life for the Jewish people that they can hardly be separated one from another: 'Each one of you shall revere your father and your mother: and you shall keep my Sabbaths: I am the Lord your God.'[5]

Many attempts have been made to summarize the most basic Jewish beliefs concerning God. Joseph Albo, the thinker and philosopher, born in Spain in 1380 C.E., maintained that the essentials of belief can be reduced to the three principles of Divine existence, Divine revelation, and reward and punishment; and that once these are accepted there is much scope to interpret God and his laws in ways that appeal to different minds.

However it may be useful to go just a little further in attempting to define the traditional rabbinic view of the

Divine. The following characteristics are accepted without reservation:

UNITY:
Judaism is totally monotheistic. There is one God, and only one God; and to him alone can prayer be addressed.

INCORPOREITY:
God is pure spirit, beyond all limitations of space, time and created matter.

OMNIPOTENCE:
God is all-powerful. All forces, natural and supernatural, are subject to his will.

ETERNITY:
God has always existed, and will always exist.

TRANSCENDENCE AND OMNIPRESENCE:
Though not a part of creation, and far above and beyond it, God is present and indwelling in all creation.

MORALITY
God is 'holy' as described elsewhere in this chapter, and requires man to imitate this quality. He is gracious and merciful, long-suffering and constant: he will reward the righteous and will punish the unrepentent wicked. It is often claimed that this concept of a 'moral God' is the principal and most original Jewish contribution to religious thought; for whilst monotheism in some form or other may have been known before Abraham, this ethical quality of the Divine was a startling innovation that revolutionized religion – compare, for example, the ethical attitudes adopted by the gods of Greece.

OMNISCIENCE:
God knows the innermost thoughts of man, and it is impossible to hide anything from him.

The above qualities, taken together, give us a view of a God who, though awful and tremendous beyond human thought and experience, is yet a personal God, ever present in everyday life and ever interested and involved in man's least activity. On this simple and straightforward concept many lives of blameless merit and true piety have been built. In each generation though, there are many who have difficulty in reconciling a concerned, personal God with the problem of evil in the world. Where, for example, was God when the Nazis burnt his Torah, and compelled those who studied it to dig their own graves? For such, the above uncomplicated view will not satisfy, and deeper levels of religious understanding must be sought, as explained elsewhere in this book.

REASON

Jewish philosophy may be regarded by some as a contradiction in terms, for the faith is based emphatically on revelation and not on conclusions reached only by the application of logical thought to experience.

However, rational thought processes are not excluded, and some can be detected in the Bible itself. Abraham is represented by the Rabbis as a rational thinker: according to a Midrash, Abraham 'discovered' God by using one of the most popular medieval philosophical proofs of God's existence. Abraham's life is compared to that of a man who on a long journey comes across a beautiful uninhabited palace: 'Is it possible that this building has no master?' asks the traveller, at which point the master makes himself known to the traveller.

Aware that views on the nature of existence are presented unsystematically in the Bible, without logical supporting arguments, later Jewish philosophers discovered a purpose for the human intellect by maintaining that the Bible exists on two levels – the simple literal level, intelligible to all; and a more profound level, discernible only by the application of pure reason in accordance with the methods of philosophy.

Rabbinic thought and writings in general, and the Talmud in particular, are not presented systematically, in logical sequence. Scholars differ as to how familiar with Greek ideas and philosophic methods were the Rabbis who compiled the Talmud, but there seems to be little evidence of direct influence.

Jewish philosophy as such can be said to have started in

the large and prosperous Greek-speaking community of Alexandria, where its best known exponent was Philo, who died in 50 C.E. According to Philo, God is entirely unknowable and indescribable: between God and the world exists an intermediate being – the LOGOS – through which God manifests himself to the world and is indwelling in it. Philo's work was of great interest to the early Christian Church, but had no lasting influence on Jewish thought.

Sa'adia Gaon, the next prominent name in Jewish philosophy, was born in 882 C.E. and was the principal of the great rabbinic academy of Sura in Mesopotamia. In several works Sa'adia attempted to convince the doubters of his own age that the religious truths transmitted by means of Divine revelation can have their validity confirmed by the exercise of pure reason. To Sa'adia, there was no conflict between reason and revelation, as both originated with God.

Ibn Gabirol, born in 1020 C.E., was the first of the Spanish school of philosophers. Between the date of his birth and that of the expulsion of the Jews from Spain in 1492, Jewish philosophy reached its zenith. It is outside the scope of this guide to describe the theories and speculations of the leading figures of that period – Solomon ibn Gabirol, Bahya ibn Paquda, Moses and Abraham ibn Ezra, Moses Maimonides, Hasdai Crescas and Joseph Albo. Most were true to their age, and akin to the 'rounded' men of the Renaissance several centuries later; they were well versed in secular knowledge and pursuits, in literature and poetry, as well as in traditional Jewish learning and mysticism.

Further developments in Jewish philosophy ceased almost entirely after the Jews left Spain, and only revived again in Germany towards the middle of the nineteenth century.

Though Jewish philosophy itself cannot be said to have had a very great influence on the development of the religion there is no doubt that Judaism has been enriched by the work of many of its philosophers – and in particular by their disciplined and systematic approach to Jewish learning as a whole, and the application of that approach to the process of codification of law and practice. Some philosophers, Maimonides in particular, are now very much more greatly valued for their work in the field of HALACHAH (the laws and observances of Judaism) than for their philosophical output: likewise it is the

Bible commentaries of the Ibn Ezras that are studied these days, rather than their works on philosophy; and men like Ibn Gabirol are remembered more for their superb Hebrew poetry than for their edifices of logical thought.

ETHICS AND LAW

The present structure of Jewish morality and law is the result of almost three thousand years of continuous development. The essential principles are held to have been handed to Moses on Mount Sinai, and are contained in the first books of the Bible – the Five Books of Moses – as well as in the parallel oral tradition. These rules were expanded and amplified in the wealth of ethical injunctions contained in the later books of the Bible. The Torah was further developed and extended between the years 450 B.C.E. and 500 C.E. by the many generations of sages whose deliberations and legislation were summarized in the Talmud – the 'classical' statement of religious, civil, criminal, social and moral law. After the completion of the Talmud, around 500 C.E., the long process of interpretation and refinement of its contents began; and this continues unabated to the present day.

As I am holy, so shall you be holy.[6]

There is no separate word for ethics in the Bible or in the Talmud. In ancient Jewish society religious practice, morality and law were all fused together into that sublime concept of 'holiness' which was stamped with the authority of the Almighty himself.

It has been told to you, O man, what is good and what the Lord requires of you. It is to do justice, to love mercy, and to walk humbly with your God.[7]

One ingredient is useless without the others; and neglect of the moral code can nullify completely the effect of the most meticulous religious observance intended to fulfil the requirement of walking humbly with God.

The standard of conduct demanded by Jewish law is

exacting. It is not Utopian in the sense of turning the other cheek; but is geared realistically to human beings, who though in some ways 'only a little lower than the angels' can in their weaker moments be overcome by evil impulses. The Rabbis had no illusions about the necessity for firm laws to regulate human behavior: 'Pray for the welfare of your government for, but for fear of the rulers, every man would devour his neighbor.'[8]

Justice is based on the often deliberately misunderstood principle of 'an eye for an eye', which was a remarkably enlightened concept for its day. As interpreted in Talmudic times it meant simply that the punishment must be carefully graded to fit the crime, and certainly must be no greater. The penalty for most crimes, therefore, was related to appropriate monetary penalties or, in other words, to a scale of fines. No one would actually have to lose an eye for blinding another; and no one could possibly be hanged or transported to Australia for the offence of stealing a sheep, which was the practice in England less than two hundred years ago.

Man is commanded to *do* justice, and to *love* mercy: the nuances of expression are important, for the opposing concepts of strict justice and mercy run together throughout the entire span of Jewish thought. Justice is stern, unbending and even harsh at times: it is impartial and is no respecter of persons or places. One cannot always love justice, even though its practice is essential for the maintenance of an ordered society. The concept of 'holiness' however requires justice to be tempered by the opposing spirit of compassion: justice and mercy must be combined together in the right proportions to sustain a harmonious moral code.

An illustration of the two opposing principles acting together is that of the stern biblical ruling that it is permissible to treat 'with rigor' a Canaanite slave, probably captured after a bout of merciless warfare. This was mitigated by the prohibition against maiming a servant, and the moral code as expressed by Job: 'If I despise the cause of my slave when he argues with me, what shall I do when God rises up... did not He that made me in the womb also make him...'[9] It developed into rules for taking care of sick and infirm slaves; and for forbidding slaves to carry out work that was degrading or unnecessary. Ill treatment of any kind was a sufficient ground to demand that a slave should be freed at once.

Even the death penalty for murder, though sometimes imposed by the Sanhedrin (Supreme Court), became so hedged with safeguards that its imposition became more and more infrequent:

> A Sanhedrin that puts a man to death once in seven years is called a murderous one. Rabbi Eleazar ben Azariah says 'or even once in seventy years'; and Rabbis Tarfon and Akiva added, 'if we had been in the Sanhedrin, no death sentence would ever have been passed'. . . .[10]

Though by the time the above was written the Roman occupiers of Palestine had already deprived the Sanhedrin of its power to inflict capital punishment, it still serves to illustrate the sentiments of the foremost Jewish sages of almost two thousand years ago, and is indicative of the way that the practice of capital punishment had developed since earlier times: the rabbis mentioned by name in the above quotation from the Talmud were no isolated idealists, but were prominent amongst those who formulated the Jewish law as we now understand it.

The Jewish legal system embraces all aspects of civil, criminal and religious law; and the moral code is intended to apply to man's every intention and action. It is often hard to separate one from the other, as the laws themselves are based on the idea of righteousness, with their emphasis on the protection of the poor and underprivileged, and their concern for human rights and dignity. Any attempt to separate the unenforceable ethical principles from laws administered by courts of justice must start with the teaching that it may be unfair in certain circumstances to insist on full legal rights, without regard for fairness and compassion. The Rabbis praise the successful litigant who chooses not to accept the full damages properly awarded to him in a court action against a poor adversary.

When challenged to summarize the whole of the Torah while standing on one foot, Hillel (first century B.C.E.) said:

Whatever is hateful to you, do not do to your neighbour. This is the essence of the Torah; the rest is commentary. Now, go and learn.[11]

That, of course, was a paraphrase of part of the commandment to be found in Leviticus, the third book of the Bible:

You shall not take revenge, nor bear any grudge; but you shall love your neighbour as yourself; I am the Lord.[12]

Rabbi Akiva (50–135 C.E.) also expressed the belief that this is the essence of the Torah; and Ben Azzai observed that the command to love one's fellow was merely a logical extension of the belief that man is made in the image of God.

There is one and the same law for you and for the resident stranger in your midst, a law binding on your descendents for all time: you and the alien are alike before the Lord.[13]

Laws and morality apply equally to Jew and non-Jew alike, and all men must be treated with fairness. The story is told of the disciples of Rabbi Simon ben Shetah (90 B.C.E.) who had bought an ass from a pagan Arab as a present for their master: on the beast's neck they found a precious jewel, which they thought of selling in order to relieve their master's poverty. Rabbi Simon indignantly refused to accept the gem on hearing that the Arab had not known about it when agreeing to the bargain, saying that he would rather hear a heathen praise the God of the Jews than gain all the treasures of this world. The lesson to be learnt from that simple tale is that a fraud against a gentile is considered to be a more serious moral offence than one against a Jew, as it involves the desecration of God's name, which is the gravest of sins.

I should have denied the One above if I rejoiced at the destruction of him that hated me, or exulted that evil overtook him.[14]

The command to love one's fellow man is further illustrated by the parable of God's rebuking the angels who were rejoicing at the drowning of the pursuing Egyptian army in the Red Sea, after the Israelites had passed safely over on dry land: 'How can you celebrate', God is pictured as saying, 'when my creatures are being destroyed?' That lesson has been carried into the synagogue service; for on the latter days of Passover only half the usual number of psalms of rejoicing known as the HALLEL are recited for that very reason.

Whoever hates any man hates Him who spoke and the world came into existence.[15]

Love of one's fellow man includes a tender care for his self-respect. The act of destroying a man's reputation by slander or malicious gossip is compared by the Rabbis to the act of murder; and it is considered a grave offence to put a fellow human being to shame in public 'so that the red leaves his cheeks', that is, as if the blood were draining out of his body after killing with a knife. One is urged to be specially careful not to risk hurting the feelings of converts by referring to their origins; and one should not embarrass a reformed criminal by alluding to his past misdeeds. The poor have a right to demand assistance; and charity must be dispensed with tact and sensitivity. It is not considered sufficient merely to give money; and emphasis is put on the duty of constructive aid to enable the recipient to provide for his own needs. Interest on personal loans is forbidden on the grounds that one should not benefit from extending help, and that one person's difficulty should not cause the enrichment of another.

The Jewish legal and ethical system deals at length with topics such as business practice and conditions of employment. Hours of work and minimum rates of pay were strictly regulated by ancient law, and any encroachment on the workers' living standards was forbidden; but slacking at work and taking unjustified time off, even for prayer, were also regarded as forms of theft. The moral conduct of business affairs is required to be of a high standard: unfair competition, cornering the market, all kinds of deceit and tricks of the trade, taking advantage of ignorance or defencelessness – these are only some of the many practices which are specifically condemned, even though they may not always be capable of being challenged at law. Care for one's fellow creatures also extends to the animal world. It is forbidden to sit down to a meal before having first made sure that one's animals have been fed. Chapter nine on 'The Home' describes the traditional method of the ritual slaughter of animals for food, which was developed from the early biblical laws so as to lessen the suffering of the unfortunate beasts by killing them in the most humane way possible.

The bulk of Jewish civil and criminal law is no longer strictly relevant to most Jews, who are obliged to live under the authority of the legal systems of their countries of residence – even though the strictly observant will still have their internal civil disputes settled by a Beth Din (rabbinic court) rather than submit them to secular jurisdiction. There is however no excuse for neglecting the moral code, the main principles of which have been outlined in this chapter, for the Jewish people has the privilege of having inherited an ethical system that is second to none.

HUMAN LIFE AND THE WORLD TO COME

Know then thyself, presume not God to scan:
The proper study of mankind is man.
Placed on this isthmus of a middle state
A being darkly wise, and rudely great,
. . .
In doubt to deem himself a god or beast.[16]

The above quotation from the work of the eighteenth-century English poet Alexander Pope touches very neatly on the traditional Jewish attitudes to man and God. Mainstream Judaism is a practical faith, concerned chiefly with man and this world; and content on the whole to leave vague and unspecified those matters which lie beyond the reach of direct human knowledge.

Two extreme views of life are expressed in the Bible. At his worst man is an animal: in fact he is '. . . like the beasts that perish'.[17] But at his best man is only slightly lower than the celestial beings: '. . . you have made him little less than the angels, crowning him with glory and honour'.[18] The choice is open to each individual: he may aspire to reach almost to the level of the angels by observing the teachings of the

Torah; or he may sink towards the level of the animals by disregarding God's commandments.

It is stated in the Bible that man was created in the image of God. That, and man's potential for good, renders human life itself sacrosanct. The life of any one man is as important to God as the whole work of creation; and he who kills one man is regarded as if he kills the entire world. The Rabbis teach that Adam was created alone in order to emphasize this very point. The extreme reverence that Judaism attaches to human life is a theme that recurs constantly throughout the whole range of Jewish thought, law and practice.

The early books of the Bible make little or no distinction between man and his soul, and seem to regard both as one and the same. Though traditional Jews hold that belief in the immortality of the soul is implicit in the Torah, comparatively few passages can be quoted to support this view. Perhaps that reticence was caused by the need to wean the Israelites from idolatrous beliefs acquired in Egypt, a country where the cult of the dead often tended to overshadow the needs of the living: Moses, it will be remembered, was originally an Egyptian prince. Though the later books of the Bible do refer to the after-life more openly, it is only in the writings of the Rabbis that reference to this belief first became explicit. The 'world to come' was described as the place where all the inconsistencies, anomalies and injustices of this world are put straight; or to quote Maimonides, it is a place 'Where God rewards those who keep His commandments, and punishes those who break them.' There is no literal 'heaven' or 'hell', only a closeness to, or a distance from God.

This concept was developed further with the belief that all souls have already been created by God: they are pure and immortal, and spend only a brief interlude in this world. The first prayer recited by the observant Jew every morning of his life is:

My God, the soul with which you have endowed me is pure: You have created it: You have breathed it into me: You will hereafter reclaim it: and You will restore it to me in the world to come.[19]

The belief in the pre-existence of all souls led the Rabbis

to recount that when God gave the Torah to the Jewish people on Mount Sinai, he gave it not only to the generation that had just left Egypt, but also to the souls of future generations yet unborn, who were similarly gathered round the foot of the mountain. Jewish mystics further extended belief in pre-existence and immortality to belief in GILGUL (transmigration, or reincarnation), in which the soul of a dead person may reappear on earth in another human form – though this never became a universally accepted doctrine in Judaism.

According to Jewish teaching the duty of man is to coop-erate with God in order to achieve his grand design. This is to be done principally by imitating his ways.

> As He is merciful, so you shall be merciful:
> as He is gracious, so you shall be gracious:
> as He is righteous, so you shall be righteous.[20]

The ultimate aim of all human activity is to establish the Kingdom of God here on earth – 'Pie in the sky, when you die' is definitely not a Jewish point of view. The Kingdom of God is visualized as a spiritual and moral Utopia. Belief in the ability of man to perfect himself in stages until the world can finally be redeemed with Divine help is a fundamental principle of faith:

> I believe with perfect faith in the coming of the Messiah; and though he may tarry, daily will I await his coming.[21]

The MESSIAH (Anointed One) is conceived as a human (and mortal) descendant of the House of David, under whose lead-ership the exile of the Jewish people from their Holy Land will finally be ended. In the new age that will then start, a great wave of moral and spiritual perfection will influence the whole of mankind into becoming true subjects of the world-wide Kingdom of God then to be established. In the messianic age, to quote the prophet: 'The Lord shall be King over all the earth. In that day the Lord shall be one and His Name one.'[22]

The ambition of a small nation such as the Jewish one to become the instrument for the redemption of the entire human race may seem presumptuous, to say the least. This hope can however be better understood when it is realised that many concepts of God, of morality and righteousness now held by large sections of the world's population were originally transmitted to them by means of this same people.

After the messianic age, God's ultimate purpose will be fulfilled, following the resurrection of the dead and the Day of Judgment:

> I believe with perfect faith that there will be a resurrection of the dead at a time when it shall please the Creator, blessed be His Name.[23]

This final consummation, leading to the 'world to come', is simply regarded as a principle of faith; and has not been subjected to detailed definition and analysis. On the whole, Judaism is content to concentrate on attempting to establish perfection here on earth; and does not try to peer through the veil that cloaks these impenetrable mysteries.

The Rabbis use the words HA-OLAM HABAH (the world to come) in two senses: in one sense it is the place to which the soul goes on the death of the body; and in the other it is the spiritual existence that will follow the Day of Judgment. Jewish concepts of the hereafter are impossible to summarize, because only belief in reward and punishment is basic. The Rabbis permitted great scope to their individual imaginations when attempting to picture the after-life. To some, the souls of the wicked are punished for up to one year before they are allowed to join the souls of the righteous in Paradise: to others the souls of the righteous go to GAN EDEN (the Garden of Eden, or Paradise), while the souls of the wicked go to GEHINAM (the 'abyss' or hell); and to others, the souls of the wicked are destroyed utterly. Likewise opinions vary on what actually happens in 'the world to come'. One rather pleasing Talmudic passage emphasizes tranquility: 'In the world to come there is no eating or drinking, no begetting of children or bargaining, no jealousy, no hatred and no strife. The righteous all sit with crowns on their heads, enjoying the light of the Divine Presence.'[24]

The preoccupation of some medieval Christian theologians with detailed descriptions of Heaven and Hell is not echoed by Jewish sources. A simple Hasidic story on which to leave this subject assumes that as study of the Torah is the ideal occupation of mankind in this world, it will be the only occupation in the world to come: for those who love the Torah, it will be Heaven. For those who hate the Torah, it will be Hell. The choice is with each individual.

THE CHOSEN PEOPLE

The Bible relates how Abraham was chosen by God:

> Leave your own country, your kinsmen and your father's house; and go to a country that I will show you. I will make you into a great nation, and will make your name great. You shall be a blessing. . . .[25]

Abraham obeyed the call promptly, and started on the long journey. It was a profoundly significant voyage of religious discovery that led to the acceptance at Mount Sinai of that core of Divine teaching which, during the subsequent course of history, was to develop as the foundation for three of the principal faiths of mankind (Judaism, Christianity and Islam), and through which nearly two thousand million human beings presently derive their notions of God, of morality, and of ethical behavior. It was also a tremendous physical journey that led Abraham himself from Mesopotamia to Canaan; and took his descendants through the period of enslavement in Egypt to their promised land; and thence after some twelve centuries of turbulent occupation, into almost two thousand years of weary and agonizing exile, ending only in the year 1948 when a surviving remnant succeeded in re-establishing the tiny independent State of Israel.

The Bible tells how the descendants of Abraham, Isaac and Jacob were blessed by God because of the exceptional merit of those three patriarchs; and how, because of this merit, the Israelites were redeemed from their life of slavery in Egypt. From that time on, though, the concept of the 'chosen people' became double-edged. At the foot of Mount Sinai, by freely accepting the yoke of the Torah, the Jewish people – so to speak – exchanged their previous bondage to Pharaoh for future bondage to God. A rabbinic parable describes how

God originally offered his Torah to all the peoples of the earth; and how each in turn rejected it because of the heavy burden involved, save for the small and previously insignificant people of Israel.

Jews believe, therefore, that God chose them as the vehicle for his revelation to mankind: 'You shall be for Me a kingdom of priests, and a holy nation.'[26] They also believe that, by accepting his commandments, the Jews also chose God: 'How odd of God, to choose the Jews. Oh no it's not, the Jews chose God.'[27] Furthermore they are taught that those two acts of choice are essentially dependent, one on the other: 'If you will listen to My voice and keep My covenant, then you shall be My own treasure from among all the peoples.'[28]

Unfortunately, as the prophets of ancient Israel were not slow to point out, God's covenant was not always kept and the people were repeatedly punished for such lapses. The Rabbis teach that the 'chosen people' continue to be punished in every age for failing to live up to the special obligations that they have undertaken – though God's unbounded love continues to sustain them, even in the depths of the suffering inflicted upon them.

It should be realized therefore that there are no arrogant overtones of a 'master race' in the Jewish concept of a chosen people. Any sincere convert, regardless of background, race or color, is accepted by Judaism, and is regarded as a true 'son' (or daughter) of Abraham. King David himself was descended from the convert Ruth. The term 'chosen' is applied to a people who, because of a highly developed religious and moral sensitivity, freely chose to undertake heavier obligations to their God than those accepted by much of mankind – and being all too human, they often fail in their endeavors. Nevertheless the Jews do rejoice in what they regard as the special relationship between them and the Divine. They are taught to believe that, despite constant backsliding, the relationship still holds; and pious Jews continue to try to do their very best to lead such lives as to fulfill their ultimate ambition of becoming 'a light unto the nations'.

THE GENTILES

According to Jewish teaching all men are required to observe the basic laws given by God to Noah, when the earth was renewed after the Flood. These fundamental rules of behaviour, deduced by the Rabbis from the biblical text, are known as the NOACHIDE laws (or the laws of Noah); and can be grouped under seven main headings:
1. Prohibition of idolatry.
2. Prohibition of blasphemy.
3. Prohibition of murder.
4. Prohibition of incest.
5. Prohibition of theft.
6. Prohibition of eating any part of a living animal.
7. The obligation to establish courts of justice.

Jews are under an obligation to teach pagans and idolaters to conform to these fundamental standards of conduct; but are under no obligation to persuade unbelievers to become Jews. Indeed conversion to Judaism is neither encouraged nor made easy. In no way does Judaism attempt to insist that the rest of mankind must accept its own special and particular 'knowledge' of God: it is sufficient that idolatry, murder, incest, etc. are suppressed, and that people live in ordered societies under the rule of laws administered by courts of justice.

Though Judaism has produced its full share of extreme views in many matters, it has always maintained without dissent that salvation is not reserved exclusively for Jews, and that 'the righteous of all nations have a share in the world to come'.[29]

The term 'righteous of all nations' is generally understood to include all those who observe the Noachide code – though interestingly enough Maimonides (in the twelfth century) held that to qualify for salvation the laws of Noah have to be obeyed because of religious conviction, and not merely from natural inclination. Both Islam and Christianity are regarded as conforming to the Noachide laws; and there is thus no conflict between Judaism and its 'daughter' faiths. Consequently Judaism, though often criticized for being excessively inward-looking, does have the positive virtue of concerning itself mainly with its own progress, and of not trying to coerce its neighbors into following in its precise path.

Judaism has long ceased to be a missionary faith; and those seeking to become Jews may be rebuffed on first approach with a harshness that can cause distress. In an increasingly secular world the Rabbis have much difficulty in maintaining religious standards among Jews who do have an obligation to obey the commandments of the Torah. Those who are not Jewish have no such obligation and are free to serve God in their own different ways. As the guardians of Judaism, traditional rabbis will only consider for conversion those who can prove beyond reasonable doubt their belief in the Torah and their willingness to live their future lives in accordance with its requirements. The wish to marry a Jewish partner is certainly not sufficient in itself, and indeed casts doubt on the sincerity of the motive behind the request for conversion. Rabbis are often criticized for their inflexibility in the matter of conversion for marriage, and for the suffering that can be caused by their strictness. However, the logic of a faith based on Divine revelation is as simple as it is unbending. A person wishing to join a particular club must expect to convince the committee that he or she intends to obey its rules, even though many of the existing members may be lax in their own practices. When it is believed that the rule book was written by Almighty God, the Creator of heaven and earth, then it is perhaps understandable that there is long and serious hesitation before allowing an outsider to undertake so heavy a set of obligations. Conversion to traditional Judaism is only possible after several years of study, which includes periods of living in a strictly observant Jewish environment. Once admitted to Judaism, however, the former convert is a full member of the faith, equal in every way to those who were born to it. Conversion to the 'progressive' forms of Judaism is much easier; however, such converts are not accepted as Jews by the mainstream faith, or by the State of Israel.

THE LAND OF ISRAEL

The Jewish people, their faith and their land have been inextricably connected since earliest times, to the extent that it is difficult to think of one in isolation without the others.

The Bible describes how Abraham was summoned by God to quit the corrupt society of Mesopotamia in order to travel to the land promised to his descendants, and in which the one true God could be worshipped without impediment. The land was abandoned temporarily when Jacob and his family moved to Egypt during a time of famine, and then stayed on to become enslaved by subsequent Egyptian kings. After gaining their freedom from the Egyptians, and receiving the Torah from God, the people once again entered into occupation, first vanquishing the original inhabitants. The successes and failures of the next twelve hundred years are well documented in the Bible, and are also referred to occasionally in outside sources. The Temple in Jerusalem was finally destroyed by the Romans in 70 C.E.; and with the disastrous crushing of the last Jewish revolt against Roman rule in 135 C.E. the remaining vestiges of Jewish self-government were extinguished, and the people's grip on the land began forcefully to be relaxed.

The next heavy blow to fall upon the Jewish population of what then was Roman Palestine was the Emperor Constantine's conversion to Christianity in 313 C.E.. Christianity became the religion of the State, and Jews suffered as religious heretics as well as political malcontents. The number of Jews and their influence declined progressively during the Christian period, and few were left in the Holy Land to witness the Arab conquest of the seventh century.

Hearing of the atrocities committed by the Crusaders in Europe (eleventh to thirteenth centuries), the Jewish communities of the Holy Land helped the Arabs to defend Jerusalem; and were massacred without mercy by the conquering armies. The eventual return of the Moslems brought some relief; and for the next few centuries the size and fortune of the small Jewish population alternately waxed and waned in response to internal conditions and to external stimuli. The onset of political Zionism in the latter part of the nineteenth century led to a gradual build up of the Jewish community of Palestine, culminating in the declaration of the independent State of Israel in 1948.

The leadership and development of the Jewish faith gradually shifted from the Holy Land to Babylon during the years of Roman and Christian oppression. The Jerusalem Talmud was finished in the latter half of the fourth century C.E.; and the last of the Palestinian academies, in Tiberias, was closed in 421 C.E. The ascendancy of the great religious academies of Babylon was then unchallenged; and their master work, the Babylonian Talmud, spread its influence over all the Jews of the diaspora (dispersion).

The sixteenth century saw a revival of religious leadership in the Holy Land. Many scholars settled there; and Safed in particular became the center of mystical and rabbinic teaching, with personalities such as Joseph Caro, Isaac Luria, and Moses Cordovero in residence. However until modern times when Israel has again become the most important religious center, it would be fair to say that most of the formative developments in Judaism were achieved by the Jews of the diaspora.

During the many centuries of their long exile Jews never ceased to yearn for the promised return to their Holy Land. Only in the land of Israel is it possible to obey God's commandments to the full – for many laws of the Torah, particularly those relating to agriculture, can only be observed in the Land. The Bible often introduces a law with the words, 'And it shall come to pass when you come to the land'. For this reason the Jewish people, in their dispersion, developed a form of worship in which the centrality of Zion was never forgotten.

> By the rivers of Babylon we sat down and wept when we remembered Zion. . .
> How could we sing the Lord's song in a strange land?
> If I forget you, O Jerusalem, let my right hand wither away;
> Let my tongue cleave to the roof of my mouth if I remember you not,
> If I set not Jerusalem above my highest joy.[30]

That lament of the early exiles in Babylon neatly summarizes the unique blend of religious and national sentiment which lies at the heart of the age-long love of Zion. Jews turn towards Jerusalem when they address God in prayer; they are often buried together with a fragment of soil from the Holy Land; they lovingly recount details of the former Temple rituals in their daily services; and they never cease to implore God to inaugurate the messianic age, when their exiles will return 'from the four corners of the world'. During times of trouble and persecution the Passover prayer 'Next year in Jerusalem' assumes particular poignancy.

The ambition to end one's days in the Holy Land is one that was often fulfilled by pious Jews, who journeyed to Jerusalem in their old age for that purpose. It was only in the last century that philanthropists such as Sir Moses Montefiore, Baron Maurice de Hirsch, Baron Edmond de Rothschild and others took the first practical steps to improve the lot of Palestine's Jewish inhabitants by enabling them to sustain themselves on the land by their own efforts. Severe persecution of Jews in Russia towards the end of the nineteenth century, coupled with the realization that Jews could expect little from a Europe steeped in hatred, led directly to the birth of political Zionism. The Zionist movement, which aimed at a physical return of the mass of the Jewish people to the historic land of Israel, was at first resisted by many of the well-established Jews of western Europe, who saw in it a threat to their continued well-being in the countries of their adoption. However the tragic events which overtook the Jewish population of Europe during this century served to sweep aside most doubts, and precipitated the chain of events that led in 1948 to the establishment of an independent Jewish State in part of the original Holy Land, west of the river Jordan.

The first act of the new State of Israel was to abolish all restrictions on Jewish immigration, thus permitting the start of the long-awaited 'ingathering of the exiles'. The subsequent 'Law of Return' confirmed the right of all Jews to settle in their ancestral homeland, regardless of economic circumstances, cultural background or skin color. The first to benefit were the wretched survivors of the European holocaust during which an estimated six million Jews were foully murdered. Next to follow were the ancient Jewish communities of the Near East, driven from their homes by the rising tide of Arab nationalism and militant Islam. During the first twenty years or so of its existence the new State welcomed and resettled over 600,000 Jews from Europe, a similar number from Arab lands, and others from North and South America, South Africa, and elsewhere. The flow of Jews to the Holy Land continues, and now includes people from the Soviet Empire – though sadly in fewer numbers. Some of Israel's efforts to rescue whole communities were truly spectacular – such as Operation Magic Carpet which brought Jews from medieval conditions in Yemen to twentieth-century Israel; and the more recent Operation Moses which saved part of a very primitive tribe of black Ethiopian Jews (the Falashas) from the persecution of their Christian neighbors and the even more urgent ravages of famine.

Some small groups of religious Jews still maintain that the establishment of a secular State is an impious act. They refuse to recognize modern Israel and its laws, believing that Israel can only be re-established by God in the messianic age. But the overwhelming mass of the people see the rebirth of Israel in terms of an abiding miracle which their generation has been privileged to witness. For them, Israel can never be just another small country of the Middle East; and their emotional ties are deep and enduring.

6

Torah

INTRODUCTION

Properly translated into English as 'teaching', Torah is also commonly referred to as 'the Law'.

The word Torah is used in two ways. In the narrow sense it is simply the Five Books of Moses (Genesis, Exodus, Leviticus, Numbers and Deuteronomy), Divine in origin and unchallengeable in authority – the sacred scrolls that are read out and treated with such reverence in the synagogues. In its broader sense the term Torah is also taken to include the Oral Law – encompassing the entire range of Jewish religious practice and belief, law, morality and mysticism – which, according to tradition, was simultaneously made known to Moses at Sinai.

As shown by the following quotation from the Talmud, the Rabbis do not seem to have been too troubled by the apparent contradiction between the belief that the oral tradition was revealed on Mount Sinai, and its subsequent development over thousands of years:

> . . . when Moses ascended on high to receive the Torah, he found the Holy One, blessed be He, adding tittles (crown-like symbols) to the actual letters of the text. Moses said: 'Lord of the Universe, what is the purpose of this'. . . . He replied: 'After many generations a man called AKIVA will arise, who will elaborate many, many laws on each tittle.' 'Lord of the Universe, permit me to see him', said Moses. He replied: 'Turn around.' Moses was transported into the Academy of Rabbi Akiva, over a thousand years later, where he sat at the back of the class. He became more and more perplexed, for he could not follow the

arguments; but when a pupil asked on a certain subject, 'From what source do you derive it' and was given the answer 'It is a law given to Moses at Sinai', Moses was comforted.[1]

The entire subject matter of this guide, therefore, is Torah. Mysticism, ethics, beliefs, practices and customs are described elsewhere in the book; and so this chapter is devoted to an outline of the historical development of Torah as a system of law and ethical rules. The accuracy of the first part of the account given here is firmly accepted by traditional Judaism as an act of faith: it may not always agree with some of the views of secular scholars, who are free to propose and to discard new theories at will.

PRE-HISTORY

Archaeologists have established that Ur of the Chaldees in Mesopotamia, one of the richest and most civilized cities of the ancient world, was sacked and burnt to the ground by barbarian invaders in the year 1960 B.C.E. Whether or not it was that event which caused Abraham's family to move to Haran in the north of the country will always remain a matter for speculation; but the date does fit in well with the traditional account.

The pre-history of the Torah can be said to have started sometime after 1960 B.C.E. when Abraham and his retinue left Mesopotamia and migrated westwards across the great river Euphrates, to the relatively uncouth land of Canaan. The purpose of the journey was to seek and to serve the one true God. Such was Abraham's merit, and that of his son and grandson, Isaac and Jacob, that the descendants of those first pioneers and their many followers were rescued from slavery some eight hundred years later, to be given the Torah.

THE BEGINNING

In about 1200 B.C.E., roughly when the primitive Greeks were engaged in the Trojan war, Moses led the Hebrew tribes out of Egypt to the boundaries of the Promised Land. On the way, in the desert of Sinai, the written Torah (Five Books of Moses) and the oral Torah were revealed to Moses for transmission to the people.

It is clear from even a casual inspection of the Five Books of Moses that, though the scope of the teaching is fairly wide, a great deal of amplification is required before their possible use as a complete manual of law and morality. It was in answer to this need that the Oral Law was provided, partly to interpret, and partly to supplement the written law. One can therefore regard many of the actual paragraphs of the written Torah simply as headings for a series of laws, the details of which remain to be added later.

An interesting example of the beginnings of this process can even be seen in the written law, in one of the narrative sections of the Book of Numbers. The daughters of Zelophehad, who had died in the wilderness without sons, appealed to Moses against the ruling that they as females were to be given no part of their father's inheritance, which was to be divided between their male uncles. Moses, after communing with God, declared that the girls must share in their father's portion – thus establishing securely in law the basic principle of female inheritance.

Of course the other books of the Bible, considered by Jews to be sacred, though to a lesser extent than the Torah, record a great deal of early development. The Hebrew prophets, with their passionate concern for righteousness, emphasized as never before the unity of morality and religion: they strove to realize a vision in which first the Jews, and then the whole of mankind will come to acknowledge the rule of a just and merciful God. The wisdom, practical ethics and poetry contained in the Psalms, Job, Proverbs, Ecclesiastes and the Song of Songs added yet other dimensions to the growing oral tradition, and helped to supply many of the factors necessary for the growth of a balanced and humane legal and ethical structure.

EARLY MIDRASH (EXPOSITION)

In the period when the Greeks were engaged in their life and death struggle with the Persians at Marathon and later at Salamis, and when the Roman Republic was being founded, two former high officers of the Persian court were busy reconstructing Jewish life in Jerusalem. Ezra and Nehemiah, who had returned with many of their countrymen from enforced exile in Babylon, set about their self-appointed task with vigor. The Five Books of Moses were rescued from semi-oblivion: the text was freed from corruptions, and formally fixed. In 444 B.C.E. the practice of reading the Torah aloud regularly to the assembled people was re-established. But this time professional interpreters stood beside the reader, not only to translate difficult Hebrew passages into Aramaic – the common language of the Persian Empire – but also to reinterpret and extend the ancient laws for contemporary use.

Thus the oral tradition grew. Much further work was accomplished by Ezra's successors, the 'Scribes' or 'Men of the Great Assembly', who are credited with a great deal of innovative legislation. Some ancient laws were reinterpreted for contemporary use with greater flexibility and leniency; and new rules were introduced 'to make a fence around the Torah', in order to protect the people better from the risk of accidental transgression.

The method used by the Scribes to expand and transmit the Oral Law is known as MIDRASH (exposition) for it is based on the detailed study and exposition of texts taken from the Five Books of Moses. Midrash is divided into two main branches: a MIDRASH HALACHAH is a lesson with legal implications; and a MIDRASH AGGADAH is a lesson from which spiritual or moral lessons can be learnt. Halachah has come to mean Jewish law – 'the way in which they shall walk'; and Aggadah is pure narrative, comprising parables, homilies, sermons and the like.

Two examples are given here, one of an Aggadic, and the other of a Halachic Midrash. The first is a commentary on the biblical verse describing what happened when Noah sent a dove out of the ark to determine whether or not the great flood had subsided: '. . . and the dove came back to him in the evening; and in her mouth was an olive leaf, freshly plucked.'² The Midrash states: 'The dove said to the Almighty: "Lord of the Universe, may my food be bitter as the olive but given to me from your hand, rather than it be as sweet as honey but given by the hand of man". '³

The second example, on a legal matter, concerns the commandment forbidding work on the Sabbath. No definition of 'work' is given in the text; and in order better to understand what was intended the Rabbis directed their attention to Exodus 35, where a short passage concerning the prohibition of Sabbath labor is followed immediately by detailed instructions governing the building of the Tabernacle in the wilderness. The Oral Law deduced a particular lesson from the apparently inconsequential sequence of passages: 'Whatever tasks were required for the building of the Tabernacle comprise "work" that is forbidden on the Sabbath.' From that conclusion the Rabbis went on to derive thirty-nine principal labors and many subsidiary ones that are not allowed on the Sabbath – including sowing, plowing, reaping, baking, kindling fire and building. The process by which each of the prohibitions is established makes a fascinating study, and is typical of the legislative methods of the Oral Law.

The striking feature of all Oral Law before about 200 C.E. is that it was oral – that is, not written down, so as to avoid all risk of confusion with the written Torah, or any possible rivalry with it in the popular mind. Midrash therefore could only be transmitted from teacher to student by word of mouth, involving almost endless repetition, and remarkable feats of memory.

Alexander the Great conquered the Persian Empire in the year 333 B.C.E.; but the work of the Scribes continued in tranquil conditions for sixty more years before the country was plunged into a long period of turmoil and strife.

EARLY MISHNAH

The next few hundred years of Jewish history was the formative period for what we now understand as Judaism. It was a time of bitter conflicts. Jews fought for their national independence, first against the Seleucid Greeks, and then against the might of the Roman Empire, while simultaneously endeavoring to preserve their religious and moral identity from ever-

encroaching waves of alien culture. The main spiritual conflict within Jewry itself was the rivalry of the priestly and
aristocratic party of the Sadducees with that of the more
democratic Pharisees (who were most unfairly maligned by
early Christian writers). The Sadducees, whose faith was
based mainly on the Temple cult, denied the growing authority of the Oral Law, preferring as literal as possible an interpretation of the actual words of the written law. Fortunately
for the future of Judaism and the Jewish people, the Pharisees
triumphed in the end. Their stress on a creative and flexible
oral Torah, together with their belief in the immortality of the
soul and the coming of the messianic age, were ultimately
accepted by all.

Even within the ranks of the Pharisees, two rival schools
were to be found, one named after the saintly Hillel (who was
living in the first century B.C.E.) and the other after the
somewhat sterner Shammai. Hillel's interpretations of law
tended to be more lenient and not as closely bound to the
literal meaning of the biblical texts as those of Shammai,
whose judgments were usually more rigorous. For all their
many differences the members of the two opposing schools
were not enemies, and often met to argue out and decide
matters of contention.

Another method of developing Halachah (law) came to
prominence at this time. It eventually displaced Midrash Halachah as the leading system, even though both continued
side by side. This is known as MISHNAH, from the Hebrew 'to
study' or 'to repeat', referring no doubt to the repetitive way
in which the Oral Law had to be learnt in the absence of
written texts. The teachers of Mishnah were called the
TANNAIM, which is derived from an Aramaic word of the same
meaning. In Midrash, as we have seen, all comment is pinned
firmly to the words of a biblical text. The Mishnaic system of
legislation, though derived ultimately from the written law,
proceeded independently of the texts; and relied for its acceptance on the authority of succeeding generations of Tannaim
themselves.

The Oral Torah continued to grow in size and complexity
through turbulent times – both before and after the great
disaster of 70 C.E. when the Roman legions finally broke into
Jerusalem after almost four years of ferocious siege, burnt the

Temple to the ground, destroyed the city, and either massacred or enslaved its surviving inhabitants.

A NEW BEGINNING

Rabbi Jochanan Ben Zakkai, one of those leading Pharisees who had opposed the suicidal revolt against Roman rule, is given the credit for enabling Judaism and its Torah to survive the destruction of the Temple, which for so long had been at the heart of its religious life. The Talmud relates that Ben Zakkai, in the middle of the siege of Jerusalem, had his disciples declare that he had died of the plague. With much show of grief they carried him in a sealed coffin for burial outside the city walls. Once beyond the ring of determined defenders Ben Zakkai emerged from his shrouds and obtained audience of the Roman general, Vespasian, who was shortly to become Emperor. The rabbi asked the general for permission to go to the small town of Jabneh, and start (or possibly take over) a religious school there. What Vespasian thought of Ben Zakkai, and why he granted his petition – so bizarre a request during a brutal and as yet unresolved war – must remain a matter of conjecture. The fact is that Rabbi Jochanan ben Zakkai did start his famous academy at Jabneh, where the study of Torah was raised to a level that facilitated the even greater accomplishments of succeeding generations. Judaism became a universal faith, no longer dependent upon the Temple and the Holy Land. Even though Jerusalem could never be forgotten, for most practical purposes the Torah became a substitute for its sanctuary.

An academic Sanhedrin (Supreme Religious Court) was also set up in Jabneh, and its authority spread far outside the Holy Land. Its head, or NASI, was of royal descent, and often represented his people before the Roman governor. Jewish life was rebuilt painfully but surely, and learning flourished. The Hebrew text of the Bible was closely scrutinized, and purged of unauthentic material. A serious attempt was made to come to grips with the accumulated mass of Oral Law. This was sifted by scholars; and many conflicting opinions were either reconciled or settled one way or the other by majority vote. Rabbi Akiva, Rabbi Meir and others labored to arrange the incoherent bulk of Mishnah into some kind of system, which cannot have been easy as this was still in oral form. But progress was made, which aided its adaptation to new problems and made it easier to teach. From Jabneh also came a stream of Midrash of the highest quality, composed by such rabbis as Akiva, Judah ben Ilai and Shimon bar Yochai.

All this activity ended abruptly in the year 132 c.e. when the Emperor Hadrian tried to erect a temple to the pagan god Jupiter on Temple Mount in Jerusalem. The Jews rose up once again in furious rebellion; and the rest of Hadrian's reign was marked by savage repression, massacre and enslavement, causing many to flee the country. The academy and Sanhedrin at Jabneh were closed. Rabbi Akiva, an original instigator of the revolt, was put to death by the Romans with even more than their usual cruelty when he refused to comply with their prohibition of teaching Torah.

RABBI JUDAH THE PRINCE – THE MISHNAH

On the death of Emperor Hadrian in 138 c.e. the surviving remnant of the Jewish population of the Holy Land began painfully to pick up the shattered pieces of its former existence and to restore its institutions. Galilee became the new centre of piety, with the re-establishment there of the Sanhedrin. Its second Nasi (president, or patriarch), Yehuda ha-Nasi, or Rabbi Judah the Prince, was said to have been a personal friend of the Roman Emperor Marcus Aurelius. Such was his reputation that in Jewish circles he is simply called Rabbi (teacher).

Rabbi Judah realized that the complex structure of the Oral Law had come to depend for its survival almost entirely on the existence of a strong central religious authority such as the Sanhedrin. Though his long patriarchate was a time of peace he was probably only too well aware that this would not last for ever, and that further extended bouts of determined persecution would endanger the very survival of the Torah. He therefore chose to ignore the centuries-old prohibition against writing down the Oral Law; and took the decisive step of committing to writing his own summary of the

Halachah (law), comprising the accumulated Mishnaic work of his own and previous generations. His monumental book is known as the Mishnah. It is in six parts:

ZERAIM (seeds) deals mainly with religious laws relating to agriculture in the Holy Land, and also contains a section on prayer.

MOED (seasons) is concerned with laws for the Sabbath and festivals, and with rules for fixing the calendar.

NAHSIM (women) deals with marriage, divorce, and related topics.

NEZIKIN (damages) covers civil and criminal law; and also includes a treatise on morals, called PIRKE AVOT (Ethics of the Fathers).

KODASHIM (holy matters) covers the detailed regulations for maintaining all aspects of the Temple service; and also includes laws governing the slaughter of animals for food.

TOHOROT (purities) covers the laws of ritual impurity including those concerned with menstruation.

Though the Mishnah contained a special selection of topics and earlier rulings that accorded with Rabbi Judah's own views, it did not inhibit further discussion, as Rabbi Judah was scrupulous enough also to include divergent opinions where he thought that they were of value.

The Mishnah, written in Hebrew by the intellectual giant of his day, was a noble attempt to systemize Jewish law. It almost immediately came to be considered as second only in authority to the Five Books of Moses. However it was still not sufficient to deal adequately with so vast a topic, so the work started by Rabbi Judah continued for many hundreds of years after his death.

THE TALMUD

The decline of the Holy Land as the prime seat of learning started after the death of Rabbi Judah the Prince, when

Babylon gradually began to take over as the religious and cultural center of the Jewish people. Two of Rabbi Judah's pupils, Abba Arika (175-247 C.E.) – known as Rav, Aramaic for 'teacher' – and Samuel, each founded academies near Babylon at Sura and Nehardea; and a third college was started at Pumbeditha, a few years later. (One of Rav's most famous rulings is that Jews are obliged to obey the righteous laws of their countries of residence: 'the law of the land is the law'.)

No sooner was Rabbi Judah's Mishnah finished than the task began of extending its scope. The teachers of the Babylonian and Palestinian schools, called the AMORAIM (speakers), subjected every detail of the Mishnah to meticulous examination and comment. Their deliberations extended beyond the text, and included other teachings omitted by Rabbi Judah in his selection – called BARAITHA (outside) – such as the TOSEFTA (supplement): many works of Midrash, such as MEKHILTA, SIFRA and SIFREI, also came within the scope of their scrupulous analysis. The records of their discussions, agreements and disagreements, known as GEMARA (Aramaic for 'study' or 'completion'), were then collated and written down in Aramaic in the two centres of activity: Babylon, and Tiberias in Galilee. By about the year 500 C.E. the task was finished. The TALMUD (the Study) comprises Rabbi Judah's Mishnah and the Gemara. There are in fact two different Talmuds, the Babylonian Talmud composed in the Babylonian schools, and the Palestinian Talmud which was compiled largely in Tiberias and completed about a century before the other.

The Babylonian Talmud is much longer than its Palestinian counterpart and is considered to be superior in many respects. Its Gemara was written in a tolerant and sympathetic environment, where the leaders of the Jewish community – known as the Princes of the Captivity (or Exilarchs) – were accorded semi-royal honours by the Persian kings, and where scholarship could thrive undisturbed. The Palestinian Gemara was collected and written down in the teeth of the harsh Roman occupation of the Holy Land, made even worse by the added spur of Christian persecution which followed the conversion of the Emperor Constantine to that faith. It is the Babylonian Talmud, therefore, that is referred to as 'The Talmud'. It rep-

A PAGE FROM A STANDARD EDITION OF THE TALMUD

Tosafot   Mishnah

References to Codes   Gemara   Rashi

resents the 'classical' statement of Jewish law, practice and custom; and it is on that authority that traditional Judaism, as we now know it, is based.

The Talmud is a vast work. Though the Gemara is arranged into the same six sections as the Mishnah, it is largely unsystematic in that the same subject may be referred to in a dozen different places, often unexpected. Containing as it does an almost universal span of human knowledge – law, religion, morals, medicine, astronomy, history, etc. – and a bewildering welter of conflicting opinions that the student is left to sort out for himself, the Talmud is very difficult to read. The deliberations of the Amoraim are recorded with an extreme brevity, which on occasion amounts to a kind of 'shorthand', thus contributing to making the mastery of Talmud a lifelong task that can only be undertaken with the help of skilled teachers. To an observant Jew, study of Talmud is a religious duty for which there is no substitute. YESHIVOT (schools of Talmudic study) are packed with men, both young and old, who can conceive of no better endeavor.

Scholastic activity did not cease, even in the Holy Land, after what is referred to as 'the closing' of the Talmud. Midrash continued to be produced in the form of Aggadah (narration), and included major works like Midrash Rabba, Genesis Rabba, Tanhuma Midrashim and Pesikta Midrashim. In Babylon, the SABORAIM (reflecters) polished and explained the Gemara; and made some additions to the text.

THE GEONIM

Such is the veneration accorded to the Almighty by observant Jews that letters, manuscripts and books containing the name of God are not destroyed after use, like other waste paper, but are either buried reverently in a cemetery, or else deposited in a storage room attached to a synagogue. Hearing of the accidental discovery of the GENIZAH (hidden place) at the Ben Ezra Synagogue in Cairo, Solomon Shechter recovered and brought to the University of Cambridge a mass of ancient manuscript material. Though this occurred at the end of the last century, work still continues at Cambridge in identifying, collating, studying and publishing the fragmentary remains.

However a great deal of knowledge has already been gained of a period that was largely unknown before the discovery of the Genizah – that of the Babylonian Geonim, from about 600 to 1000 C.E.

After a short decline because of persecution following the Arab conquest in the eighth century, the condition of the Jewish population of Babylon was soon restored to much of its former glory. The Exilarch, or Prince of the Captivity, was once again accorded semi-regal honors, this time by the Caliph of Baghdad. As noted by a contemporary traveller:

> Horsemen, Jewish and non-Jewish, escort him every Thursday when he goes to visit the great Caliph: heralds go before, proclaiming 'Make way for our Lord, the Son of David, as is his due'. He is mounted on a horse and dressed in robes of embroidered silk . . . the Caliph rises and places him on a throne . . . and all the Mohammedan princes rise up before him.[4]

The heads of the colleges of Sura and Pumbeditha became the spiritual leaders of world Jewry. They were known as Geonim, the plural of GAON (excellency) the title with which each was addressed. The spread of Islam ensured that the authority of the Geonim was accepted in all lands conquered by the Moslems, from India in the East to Spain in the West.

Talmud continued to be taught in the academies; and scholars flocked from many countries to Sura and Pumbeditha. Copies of the Talmud were dispatched to other Jewish communities; and the first legal codes were compiled and circulated to aid understanding and observance. The range of the law was extended by means of the RESPONSA, which were reasoned judgments on law and practice prepared by the Geonim in answer to queries sent to them by Jews from all over the world.

The text of the Hebrew Bible was once again subjected to close scrutiny, and scribal errors were eliminated. Pronunciation of the sacred texts depended on oral tradition, as the Hebrew alphabet consists only of consonants, vowel sounds and punctuation being supplied from memory. Babylonian scholars attempted to add written vowel sounds and punctuation to the Hebrew letters, in order to standardize reading and pronunciation beyond further dispute. In the end though, it was the text prepared in the tenth century by Ben Asher of Tiberias (Palestine) that became the accepted Hebrew Bible. It is known as the Masoretic text after the MASORETES (from 'to hand down') who had prepared it.

Yet another important achievement of the Geonic period was the standardization of many prayers and forms of worship. The first complete prayer book was prepared for use in Spain by Amram Gaon in the year 860. Another was produced by Sa'adya Gaon for the Egyptian Jews some years later.

Sa'adya ben Yosef (882–942), better known as Sa'adya Gaon, was perhaps the greatest of the Geonim. In his philosophical book, 'Emunot Vedot' (Beliefs and Opinions), he attempted to reconcile reason with religion for the benefit of his generation. Sa'adya's role was crucial in combating and in ultimately defeating the Karaite movement, which at one time seriously threatened the survival of Talmudic Judaism with its rejection of the oral tradition and its insistence on the literal application of biblical laws. After the death of Sa'adya Gaon in the year 942, the Babylonian schools began their slow decline, giving way gradually to new centers of learning in North Africa, Moslem Spain, and Christian Europe.

RASHI AND THE TOSAFISTS

Rabbi Shelomo Itzhaki, affectionately known as Rashi from the first letters of his name, was born in France in the year 1040, at a time when the Jews of Europe were suffering grievous persecution at the hands of the Crusaders. Rashi studied with many of the leading rabbis of his day, including pupils of the illustrious Rabbi Gershon of Mainz, before founding his own school in Troyes, northern France. As well as much other work of value, including Bible commentary, Rashi produced a detailed and up-to-date Hebrew commentary on almost the whole of the Talmud, using French words written in Hebrew characters when there was no Hebrew equivalent. Rashi's commentary is the most frequently consulted of all such works, and is accorded the honor of being printed in the margin of all standard editions of the

Talmud. Composed with impressive insight and lucidity, and imbued with deep religious feeling, Rashi's commentary and other books have become standard works of reference.

Prominent in the next generation of teachers that followed Rashi was his grandson Rabbi Jacob ben Meir, called Rabbenu Tam ('our teacher the unblemished', after the Patriarch Jacob who is described in the Bible as unblemished). He and his contemporaries took particular pleasure in analyzing the Talmud and Rashi's commentary in fine detail. They raised ingenious and subtle objections to many of Rashi's explanations, before proposing original solutions of their own. These so-called Tosafot (supplements), composed by the pupils of Rabbenu Tam, now also appear alongside the text in printed editions of the Talmud.

Other Tosafists, whose work was published elsewhere, came from many different countries. Learned rabbis in England, before the expulsion of all Jews from that country in the thirteenth century, were also active in this field – including Rabbi Jacob of Orleans (martyred in London in 1189), Rabbi Yomtob of Joigny (martyred in York in 1190), and Rabbi Elijah ben Menahem of London, who seems to have been allowed to die of natural causes in 1284.

Although the next part of this chapter is devoted largely to a description of the stages in which the law was developed from the tenth to the twentieth centuries, it must not be forgotten that a steady output of work classified as Midrash was also appearing at the same time – much of it as elevating in its common humanity as the Italian 'Tanna debe Eliyahu' which declared:

I call upon heaven and earth to witness that whether a person be a Jew or non-Jew, bondman or bondwoman, according to the deeds he performs will the Holy Spirit rest on him.

Following the time of Sa'adya Gaon, Jewish minds were increasingly drawn to the philosophical method and to its application to the study of religious law. In complete contrast, as described elsewhere, development of the semi-secret mystical core of Judaism (the Kabbalah) was also proceeding with significant effect. And since the seventh century, a great flow of devotional poetry has much enriched the synagogue liturgy.

THE CODES

After the Tosafists the development of the Oral Law continued without pause along two main paths – that of the Legal Codes, and that of rabbinic Responsa. Though these activities proceeded in tandem, each will be described separately here.

The bulk of Jewish law and its interpretation had by then become so large as to demand some form of codification to render it intelligible to all those who were not accomplished scholars. Most of the rabbis who contributed to this work were Sephardim, or Ashkenazim who had come to live in Spain, North Africa or the Near East. An explanation often advanced for this division is that, unlike their Ashkenazi brethren who were compelled to live in the narrow ghettos of northern Europe, the Sephardim were usually able to participate fully in the general life of their countries of residence. They were too busy with their careers and with other secular pursuits to be able to devote to the study of Talmud the many years necessary for its mastery. In any event, rabbis of the Ashkenazi tradition always displayed a marked preference for the exclusive study of the Talmud, which – after the Bible – is the primary source of Jewish religious knowledge.

Rabbi Isaac of Fez (1013-1103), otherwise called Alfasi, was living and working in North Africa at roughly the same time as the Norman conquest of England. He was one of the first, outside Babylon, to produce a code of law. This was achieved by a drastic simplification of the Talmud, omitting much of the argument and all of the opinions with which he disagreed.

Rabbi Moses ben Maimon is known to Jews as the Rambam after the first letters of his name, and to the outside world as Maimonides. He was the outstanding codifier of his time, and one of the most brilliant men of the age. Born in 1135, Maimonides fled from fanatical Almohade rule in Spain, and finally settled in Cairo where he became a famous physician and the head of its Jewish community. His monumental code, the MISHNEH TORAH, one thousand chapters long, was completed before 1184. Written with deep religious feeling and with a clarity unusual at that date, it offered its readers an authoritative summary of developed Jewish law. Called the Mishneh Torah (Second Torah), because according to its author no further authorities would be needed after it to determine the law on any subject, the code was intended to be complete in itself.

The Rambam's approach to religion was guided essentially by the principles of reason; for he was an admirer of Aristotle as well as an accomplished philosopher in his own right. He possessed an acute facility which enabled him to differentiate between the fundamentals of the faith and those aspects which can be varied – in his own words – 'as a physician will amputate the hand or the foot of a patient in order to save his life'. His concept of religion was universal. He taught that the righteous of all nations are sanctified in the sight of God.

'From Moses to Moses, there has not arisen one to equal Moses.' This popular saying, illustrating that Maimonides was regarded in his own lifetime as a second Moses, did not prevent severe criticism of the Mishneh Torah – much of it justifiable. In order to present his rulings with maximum clarity the Rambam had omitted all Talmudic argument from his text. Also, he never named his sources. Even more important, when preparing his book he seems to have neglected the views of distinguished Ashkenazi scholars. Attempts were made by others to remedy some of the defects, and their comments may be found printed alongside Maimonides's own text in later editions of the Mishneh Torah.

Another influential code was that written by Rabbi Jacob ben Asher, and called the TUR ('rows', after the four rows of gems on the ceremonial breastplate of the High Priest). Jacob was the son of the famous Rabbi Asher ben Yehiel (1250–1327), known as Rosh after the first letters of his name, and also as Asheri. The Rosh, who had fled from persecution in Germany, became the Rabbi of Toledo in Spain where he produced a valuable legal commentary. His ideas are also included in the Tur, even though Rabbi Jacob's code is an original work in its own right.

Many codes were produced; but the only other to be mentioned here is the SHULHAN ARUCH (The Prepared Table), printed first in Venice in 1565. The author, Joseph Caro, was forced to quit Spain when all Jews were expelled in 1492, the year in which Columbus set sail for America. He settled in Safed in the Holy Land, from which his fame spread as a leading mystic and scholar. The result of a meticulous study of the Tur lasting for twenty years, the Shulhan Aruch is based on the works of Alfasi, Maimonides and Asheri. Where these three disagreed on any point Caro generally adopted the majority opinion. This proved to be the main failing of the Shulhan Aruch however, for the views and customs of the Ashkenazim were once again ignored. Poland had by this time become an important center of Jewish life: Rabbi Moses Isserles of Cracow wrote a MAPPAH (tablecloth) for the 'Prepared Table', stating the differing Ashkenazi opinions and customs. From that time on the Mappah was always printed alongside the text of the Shulhan Aruch; and this modified version soon became the definitive guide to Jewish law and practice that it still remains.

The formal position in Jewish law is that the further each generation gets from the revelation on Sinai the less authoritative becomes its interpretation of the oral tradition. Hence teachers of Torah are listed in descending order of seniority:

WRITTEN TORAH
The Five Books of Moses – the ultimate authority.

ORAL TORAH
The Tannaim – up to the 'closing' of the Mishnah in the third century C.E.

The Amoraim – up to the 'closing' of the Talmud in the sixth century.

The Rishonim (The First Ones) – up to the 'closing' of the Shulhan Aruch in the sixteenth century.

The Aharonim (The Later Ones) – after the Shulhan Aruch.

In practice however the principle that 'the law follows the latest ruling' usually prevails. A later master who has studied all the earlier rulings is usually deferred to by virtue of his accumulated knowledge.

RESPONSA

Law was also developed through the general acceptance of pronouncements made by individual rabbis of distinction. An early example was the devising of a legal instrument known as a 'Prozbul' by Hillel (first century B.C.E.) to circumvent the biblical law that required all debts to be cancelled each seventh year (the year of release), which was having an adverse effect on commercial activity.

As described earlier in this chapter, the Geonim of Babylon made much use of the method of Responsa to regulate Jewish life between 600 and 1000 C.E. Their work was continued by the rabbis of the medieval period, and is still employed today.

Responsa are written replies to legal queries addressed to outstanding rabbis by less learned colleagues. They deal with individual points not specifically mentioned in the Talmud or the Codes. In general each Responsum refers to a particular case brought to the attention of the rabbi concerned. It consists of a description and analysis of the sources consulted, a survey of similar problems and relevant rulings, and a final statement determining the law – in other words, what we would now describe as a reasoned judgment.

Responsa literature has had a far-reaching effect on the whole of Jewish thought and practice; and a few examples are given here. Rabbi Gershon of Mainz, born in 960 C.E. and known as 'The Light of the Exile', departed from Talmudic law by prohibiting polygamy. In similar manner he ruled also that no woman could be divorced from her husband without her consent. Rashi some years later decreed that forced converts to Christianity must be welcomed back to the Jewish faith, and should not suffer reproach or disability because of their lapse. Rabbenu Tam forbade Jews to wash their dirty linen in public by submitting civil disputes between themselves to non-Jewish courts for resolution, rather than taking them to a Beth Din (rabbinic court). In more recent times rabbis who survived the concentration camps of Nazi Europe

DEVELOPMENT OF THE TORAH

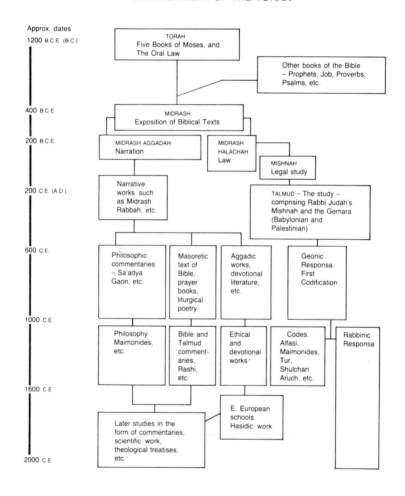

Approx. dates

1200 B.C.E. (B.C.) — TORAH — Five Books of Moses, and The Oral Law

Other books of the Bible – Prophets, Job, Proverbs, Psalms, etc.

400 B.C.E. — MIDRASH — Exposition of Biblical Texts

200 B.C.E. — MIDRASH AGGADAH Narration — MIDRASH HALACHAH Law — MISHNAH Legal study

200 C.E. (A.D.) — Narrative works such as Midrash Rabbah, etc. — TALMUD – The study – comprising Rabbi Judah's Mishnah and the Gemara (Babylonian and Palestinian)

600 C.E. — Philosophic commentaries – Sa'adya Gaon, etc. — Masoretic text of Bible, prayer books, liturgical poetry — Aggadic works, devotional literature, etc. — Geonic Responsa. First Codification

1000 C.E. — Philosophy Maimonides, etc. — Bible and Talmud comment-aries, Rashi, etc. — Ethical and devotional works' — Codes. Alfasi, Maimonides, Tur, Shulchan Aruch, etc. — Rabbinic Responsa

1600 C.E. — Later studies in the form of commentaries, scientific work, theological treatises, etc. — E. European schools. Hasidic work

2000 C.E.

had to rule on painful topics such as whether or not murder had been committed when a baby died as the result of its mouth being held closed to silence its cries to prevent the Nazis discovering the secret hiding place in a bunker of a group of Jews.

Since the acceptance of the Shulhan Aruch as definitive, Responsa became the main medium for deciding points of law not specifically covered by the Talmud or that code. It still fulfils that function, with questions such as the permissibility of certain human organ transplants, and the possibility of 'in vitro' fertilization requiring decision for those who govern their lives by the teachings of the Torah.

Of course, one individual Responsum will often differ from another in its conclusions. When this happens it is the majority view that prevails eventually and becomes law. An example of this is the furore that followed the discovery of electricity and its widespread use for lighting and heating. Is switching on a light equivalent to the biblical concept of 'kindling', forbidden on the Sabbath, or is it permissible? Initially there was much disagreement between rabbis, until a consensus was achieved forbidding the operation of a light switch as a form of 'kindling' – which is the present law. (Lights may however be turned on by the use of a pre-set time switch.)

As well as Responsa, important contributions to Torah in general emanated from the thriving centers of Jewish piety and learning in eastern Europe from the early seventeenth century onwards. These of course included those incomparable contributions to Aggadic literature in the form of the fables, legends and parables composed by the followers of Israel ben Eliezer (1700-60) – better known as the Ba'al Shem Tov (Master of the Holy Name) – which are now attracting the attention of far wider circles than ever before.

IN CONCLUSION

A twelfth-century convert to Judaism, presumably feeling insecure in a community of natural-born Jews, wrote to Maimonides enquiring whether he was permitted to address God in prayer with traditional phrases such as 'O Lord our God and God of our fathers', 'God of Abraham, Isaac and Jacob', '... who separated us and chose us', 'who brought us up out of the land of Egypt', etc. In his long reply Maimonides explained carefully that Abraham had taught his own children, his household and all people the religion of the one true God; and that:

> Every stranger who joins us to the end of time, and everyone who recognizes the unity of God as taught in scripture, is a disciple of Abraham our father.

The convert was thus instructed to use all the words of the traditional prayers, without exception – 'whether you pray in private, or whether you lead the Congregation in prayer'. Maimonides added emphatically:

> There is no difference between us and you in any way. . . .
> If our descent is from Abraham, Isaac and Jacob, your descent is from God himself. As stated by the Prophet Isaiah, 'one shall say, I am the Lord's; another shall call himself by the name of Jacob'.[5]

The above example illustrates well that, though the word 'Halachah' is usually translated as 'law', it is not restricted to the narrow sense of religious, criminal and civil legislation; but embraces within its scope almost the entire field of human behavior.

A large part of this chapter has been devoted to Halachah, partly because of the importance of its development, and partly because it is easier to deal with in outline than is the stream of Aggadah (narration) that proceeded simultaneously, often from the pens of the very same rabbis. All work of spiritual, theological, mystical and moral significance – in the form of books, Bible commentary, parables, discourses, sermons, devotional poetry and ethical wills (in which fathers handed down to their children the sum total of the wisdom accumulated during their lifetimes) – though not Halachah, is still an essential part of the same Torah in the light of which observant Jews attempt to order their lives.

7

Kabbalah

INTRODUCTION

Since the eleventh century KABBALAH (tradition) has been the word most commonly used to describe the esoteric teachings of Judaism, embracing the entire range of mystical theory and practice. This topic will be strange to most readers, as public awareness of Kabbalistic teaching has been suppressed in the West for the greater part of the past two hundred years. It was largely through the efforts of the late Gershon Sholem, on whose work this chapter is based, that general interest has once again been aroused in the mystical tradition which is one of the essential ingredients of Judaism.

In Talmudic times Kabbalah was communicated only to very small circles of the initiated, carefully chosen for their deep religious knowledge, their maturity of age and outlook, and for their piety and high ethical standards. Although knowledge of Kabbalah widened slightly in Spain during the early years of the fourteenth century, it was not until the expulsion of the Jews from that country in 1492 that its theories became a dominant spiritual force in popular Judaism. The original esoteric tendency was strongly revived following the collapse of the false Messiah Shabbetai Zvi in 1666, when Kabbalistic doctrines came to be regarded as dangerous and were suppressed. However some aspects of Kabbalistic teaching were again popularized by the spread of the later Hasidic movement in eastern Europe during the eighteenth and nineteenth centuries, and became the common property of the movement's mass following. Many Jews today may have heard of Kabbalah but are unaware of its history, teachings and influence.

Some, but by no means a majority of Kabbalists, were

practising mystics who aimed at direct personal communion with God. This was achieved by means of various forms of meditation which enabled the soul to free itself from the confines of the body in order to contemplate and experience the Divine. Mystics belonging to many other religious systems use broadly similar methods to induce ecstatic awareness but direct this to different ends. In the Jewish form of mysticism the soul always keeps its own identity, entirely separate from that of its Creator which it adores. It never seeks to merge itself with the Absolute, and never aspires to the Nirvanah of the eastern faiths. With few exceptions the masters of Kabbalah maintained the utmost discretion about their own personal mystical experiences, and only very rarely left written accounts of them.

As evolved from the time of the second Temple to the present day, the teachings known as 'Speculative Kabbalah' seek to explain the mysteries of the hidden nature of God and their relationship to man and to the world in which man lives. In Kabbalah the imperfections of this world are attributed to a 'flaw' that either followed the last act of creation, or else was built into the end of the creative process itself. It is the task of mankind to correct that fundamental 'flaw'. The Kabbalah embraces a view of existence in which each individual, and the whole community of Israel, are protagonists in a cosmic struggle between the forces of good and the forces of evil. Every Jew, through his actions and prayers, has a part to play in the Divine purposes of hastening the advent of the messianic age and of restoring the original harmony of creation.

Followers of the mystical tradition were firm believers in the powers of the spiritual world, both for good and for evil. Divine names and the letters contained in them were considered to be particularly effective in invoking the hidden forces, and were often used for that purpose in mystical meditation.

'Practical Kabbalah' is the term now used to describe all attempts to employ the powers of the spiritual world for everyday purposes unconnected with mystical experience. Such practices, even when for the public good and not for personal advantage, were strongly discouraged. They could only be performed by truly righteous individuals, and then at considerable personal risk. However the existence of an extensive ancient literature on the subject, together with many devices such as amulets, indicate that the warnings were very often disregarded in practice. Sorcery, or the attempted harnessing of the powers of darkness for selfish or harmful causes, was always strictly forbidden by Judaism. It is important to realize that there is a distinct boundary between sincere religious attempts to come to terms with the spiritual sphere and those motivated by ambition, greed or other unworthy reasons. Inevitably, perhaps, many charlatans and evil-minded people attached themselves to the fringes of Kabbalah, ignoring its true purpose and using its name as a cloak for their real intentions. Jewish folklore is permeated by memories of such people, who are largely responsible for the false and distorted impressions of Kabbalah still current today.

EARLY KABBALAH

Kabbalah has been regarded traditionally as the secret part of the Oral Torah revealed to Moses at Sinai; and comparatively few claims for originality of thought were ever made by its masters during the two thousand years of its development.

Much remains unknown about the first phase of Jewish mysticism from 100 B.C.E. to 1000 C.E. Two texts from the Bible formed the principal subjects for esoteric teaching during the second Temple period, and each became the source of distinct mystical traditions and literatures. The first chapter of Ezekiel gave rise to those speculations known at MA'ASEH MERKABAH (the Divine Chariot), and the first chapter of Genesis to those grouped under the description MA'ASEH BERESHIT (the work of creation).

Merkabah mysticism was concerned with those processes by which man's soul can ascend through the seven heavenly realms to a vision of God's Glory on the Throne/Chariot described in the Book of Ezekiel. It dealt with details of the upper worlds surrounding the Throne to which God's Glory descends from the unknown, and did not contribute any new understanding of the nature of God, or of creation.

The literature of Ma'aseh Bereshit, on the other hand,

contains a speculative Hebrew text of great influence – the SEFER YETZIRAH (Book of Creation), written in or before the sixth century C.E. The book opens with the statement that God created the world by means of thirty-two mysterious 'paths' of wisdom, and then proceeds to explain in highly symbolic and obscure terms how God called the world of creation into existence with the instruments of language. The 'paths' referred to in Sefer Yetzirah are the letters of the Hebrew alphabet plus ten SEFIROT (abstract entities, or elements, or rays? – the precise meaning of the Hebrew word remains obscure). The way was thus opened for attempts to learn the 'hidden' meanings of biblical words and phrases by comparing the numerical values contained therein with that of other key words and phrases to be found elsewhere. (There are no numbers as such in written Hebrew, and each letter of the alphabet has numerical value.) Many magical practices were also based on similar methods – known as GEMATRIA, or numerology.

MEDIEVAL HASIDISM

A strong ethical quality was introduced into Jewish mysticism for the first time by the medieval Hasidic movement of Germany in the twelfth and thirteenth centuries. Yehudah the Hasid (the Pious) who died in 1217, and his pupil Eleazar of Worms, were its best known masters, and many of their ideas are contained in the SEFER HASIDIM (Book of the Devout).

Scholarship and intellect were no longer regarded as essential factors in the make-up of a holy man. The Hasid (pious man) was able to come close to God by means of his renunciation of the ordinary life of this world in favour of an existence based on good works, prayer and contemplation. He had to be indifferent to the scorn and reproaches of the ignorant, as well as completely lacking in self-interest – 'What is mine is yours: what is yours is yours: that is the way of the Hasid'.[1] Probably because of his neglect of wordly affairs, the Hasid came to be regarded as a person of great power, able to command the hidden forces.

The Hasidic movement to some extent moved in parallel to

similar developments within the medieval Church. Common factors included many of the ideas on penitence, the sexual imagery of the mystical poetry, and the ideal lives of the holy men – except that the monk was celibate, while the Hasid maintained a full sex life within marriage.

THE ZOHAR

It was in the sometimes gentler and more tolerant southern regions of Europe that speculative Kabbalah struck the deepest roots in the minds of Jewish religious thinkers. From the twelfth century onwards, starting in Provence and then spreading to Spain, Kabbalistic theories rapidly developed a new profundity and coherence. They came to encompass the very nature of human existence, and sought to explain how the hidden, unknown and unknowable God manifests himself in the world of creation – how the gulf is bridged between the Infinite and the finite.

The appearance of the SEFER HA ZOHAR (Book of Splendor) at the end of the thirteenth century was the crowning achievement of Spanish Kabbalah. Copies of the book were first circulated by Moses de Leon of Castile, who claimed to be in possession of the original manuscript written by Shimon bar Yochai. (Following the crushing of the revolt against Roman rule in Palestine in the year 135 C.E., Shimon was sentenced to death by the Romans. He spent the next twelve years with his son hidden in a cave where, according to tradition, he was visited each day by the Prophet Elijah and was taught those 'mysteries' which constitute the subject matter of the Zohar.) Opposing the traditional belief, the late Professor Gershon Sholem amassed evidence to demonstrate that the entire Zohar was the work of Moses de Leon himself. Others think that Moses de Leon compiled the Zohar from a variety of more ancient sources. The book takes the form of a collection of commentaries on parts of the Torah, the Song of Songs and the Book of Ruth. It deals with the nature of the Divine, of man's soul, of good and evil, and of the final redemption: some of its leading ideas will be outlined later in this chapter. Knowledge of the Zohar gradually spread throughout the entire Jewish world during the three hundred years after its first appearance, until it came to occupy a unique position, ranking close to the Talmud in its influence and authority.

THE 'HOLY LION'

The golden age of religious and intellectual achievement and of material prosperity in Spain came abruptly to an end in 1492, when all those members of the Jewish population who refused to embrace Christianity were forcibly expelled from that country. The shattered and bewildered exiles carried their sacred books with them. They increasingly turned to the Zohar for an explanation of the catastrophe, and as a key to their future redemption. Safed in Palestine, close to the tomb of Shimon bar Yochai, became the main center of Kabbalah, where the ideas expressed in the Zohar were further developed into comprehensive doctrines well suited to the mood of the exiles and to the yearning of Jewish people everywhere for the final Redemption which would bring an end to their sufferings. Of the several outstanding masters of Safed, Isaac Luria (1534-72) became the most influential because of his saintly personality and his startlingly original ideas. A legend in his own time, Luria – known popularly as Ha Ari (the Lion) – wrote no books during his short life; and all that we know of his thoughts and actions derives from the work of his disciples and contemporaries. Luria's most important ideas, which had enormous effect, are described later (see page 122). Apart from their doctrines, the mystics of Safed permanently enriched Judaism with several of their customs as well as with liturgical poems and hymns of great beauty.

From Safed, Kabbalah in general and Luria's doctrines in particular spread among Jews everywhere. Parallel to the surge of religious activity that accompanied this diffusion of mystical theory, the feeling so aptly described as 'messianic tension' also grew in intensity. Jews had been taught by the Kabbalah to view their own exile from the Land of Israel in terms of the original 'flaw' in the act of creation. They had been encouraged to long for the final Redemption, heralded by the coming of the Messiah, and to work and pray for that consummation in their own lifetime. Major catastrophes, such as the expulsion from Spain, began to be seen in the light of 'the birth pangs of the Messiah'. Later in 1648, a terrible disaster overtook the affluent and semi-autonomous Jewish community of Poland and Lithuania, which by then had become the focus of Ashkenazi learning and culture. A revolt by Cossacks and peasants against Polish rule in the Ukraine, led by Bogdan Chmielnicki, led to a series of ferocious massacres of Jews on a scale then unsurpassed in European history. (The Jews had previously taken a leading part in the colonizing of the Ukraine by Poland.)

THE FALSE MESSIAH

Scholars may differ about the extent to which each of the above factors influenced what followed; but it is not disputed that the proclamation of Shabbetai Zvi as Messiah, at Gaza in 1665, prompted an unprecedented wave of penitence and rejoicing throughout the Jewish world. From Kurdistan and Persia to Poland and Russia, in cities ranging from Smyrna and Constantinople to Amsterdam and Hamburg, rabbis and laymen, rich and poor, all joined in an extraordinary outburst of messianic enthusiasm; and began to make practical preparations for their imminent departure for the Holy Land. A fuller account of this fascinating yet tragic episode lies outside the scope of this book, but it has been well documented elsewhere.

Large numbers of Shabbetai's followers maintained their faith in his mission even after he abandoned Judaism in favor of Islam on command of the Sultan. They believed that his apostasy was a secret part of the Divine plan with mystical purpose, and that he would eventually 'return' to fulfill his role as King Messiah. When this event failed to occur, most turned away from Shabbetai Zvi with revulsion, and did their best to eradicate all traces of his influence and to blot out the very memory of his name. A few persisted in their belief, in secret, despite severe persecution. One scholar believes that these events influenced those tendencies towards 'enlightenment' and reform that appeared in Judaism during the years following the French Revolution. Other messianists developed increasingly anarchic theories and bizarre practices, and formed themselves into heretical sects, far beyond the limits of Jewish tolerance. A remnant of the Frankist sect, some of whose adherents outwardly joined the Catholic Church, survived as a coherent group until the middle of the nineteenth century. The Doenmeh sect, which outwardly professed Islam, remained strongly established in Salonika until the population of that city was dispersed following the war between Greece and Turkey in 1924.

After the collapse of Sabbatianism, what can be described as 'orthodox' Kabbalah turned its back on the masses. It once again became the preserve of a select few, as it had always been before being swept along on the great tide of popular messianic fervor. Traces of a living Kabbalah, with its practices of mystical prayer and contemplation, survive in this form to the present day.

EAST EUROPEAN HASIDISM

The other and more vigorous successor to Kabbalistic tradition was the later Hasidic movement of eastern Europe, founded by Israel ben Eliezer (1700–60), the Ba'al Shem Tov (Master of the Holy Name). This popular mass movement represented a reaction against what was considered to be the dry scholastic attitudes of traditional rabbinic Judaism, and appealed more to the feelings and emotions of its followers than to their intellects. The doctrines of the Hasidim were derived directly from Lurianic Kabbalah, but with differing shades of meaning and emphasis. Its impetus came from the uneducated common people, afflicted by poverty and repression.

The most original feature of Hasidism was the appearance of a series of saintly figures of charismatic personality. Each TZADDIK (righteous man), or REBBE (teacher), attracted a large circle of followers who lived in close contact with him, and who looked to him for practical advice on everyday living as well as for religious inspiration. Many of the original Tzaddikim founded dynasties, some of which flourish in the United States, Israel and England to the present day. Two of the best known of these groups are the inward-looking Satmar, and the outward-looking Lubavitch (which tries actively to reawaken religious interest among assimilated Jews).

The wealth of legend, literature and wisdom produced by the Hasidim has lately become known to much wider circles through the work of writers such as Martin Buber. Its value is also gaining appreciation in the non-Jewish religious world.

DOCTRINES

Two main difficulties stand in the way of a lucid account of the ideas and doctrines of the Kabbalah. The first is that of language. When seeking to describe thoughts and experiences which go to and even beyond the limits of normal human comprehension, plain language can no longer serve; and the Kabbalists have been driven to express themselves in an obscure language of their own. This is studded with symbols, myths and allegories; and is very difficult for outsiders to understand. Many of its expressions will appear strange and startling to modern readers at first sight. They must be regarded primarily as symbols, intended to convey glimpses of the partly inexpressible meanings which lie behind them. The second barrier to any concise 'explanation' of Kabbalah is the sheer complexity of the subject, which contains many different and often paradoxical theories of the nature of existence. The following paragraphs are intended to provide a first impression of what Kabbalistic thought is about, focusing on the world of the Zohar in the early part of the sixteenth century, and on Isaac Luria's subsequent innovations.

The Infinite

All Kabbalistic systems stem from the same basic belief in the nature of the Divine. There is a fundamental barrier between the world in which we live and the Infinite. The word 'God', in this context, is used in two different senses. In one sense 'God' represents the absolute reality – often called EN-SOF (Infinite) – which must always remain entirely beyond the range of human comprehension, and about which all speculation is futile. In its other sense 'God' represents a 'projection' from En-Sof (the hidden God) into the finite world of creation – in other words, the personal God of the scriptures. The Divine can only be perceived through that aspect which is accessible to human thought. It is important to realize that when we speak of God's wisdom, God's compassion, etc. we are in no way referring to En-Sof (the unknown and unknowable God), but only to its particular projection or manifestation in our world.

Put another way, there are two Divine spheres: the first is that of En-Sof, concealed from all but itself; and the second, springing from the first, is the one through which (because of its relationship with the created world) it becomes possible to know God. One sphere proceeds from the other and forms a perfect unity with it – to quote the Zohar, very much as flames proceed from a piece of burning coal.

The Sefirot

The method by which God emerged from the depths of himself into creation is one of the principal topics of Kabbalistic thought. Being infinite and absolute, nothing can exist outside En-Sof; and the world as we know it must somehow have been contained within En-Sof. However the masters of the Kabbalah did not believe that our own imperfect and finite world could possibly have proceeded directly from En-Sof. Their systems postulate ten Sefirot (attributes of God, 'spheres', or sapphire-like 'rays') as the means by which God bridges the gulf between the Infinite and the finite universe. In the words of the Zohar:

> From the depths of His Infinite Being, He projected ten successive channels of light (the Sefirot), through which He became manifest (revealed) in the finite world.

The symbolism used to describe the world of the Sefirot is very involved. A brief description is given here for the sake of completeness; but it is realized that this will not be very meaningful to the casual reader. The Sefirot emanate from each other in fixed sequence, but also contain the qualities of each other in different degrees. They all combine to form one great unity with En-Sof and with the lower world of creation. They comprise a group of active (masculine) powers, a group of passive (feminine) powers, and a third group springing from the other two. Together they are balanced in a perfect harmony which sustains creation.

TREE OF DIVINE POWER

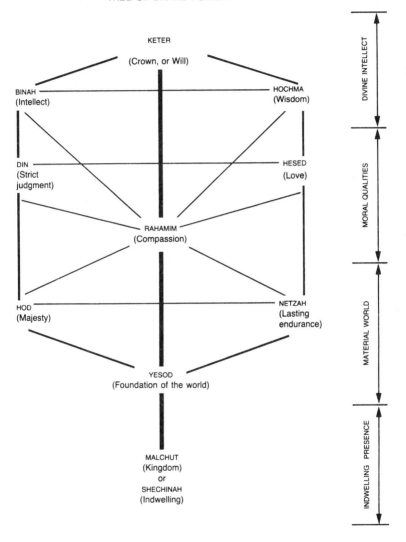

KETER
(Crown, or Will)

BINAH
(Intellect)

HOCHMA
(Wisdom)

DIN
(Strict
judgment)

HESED
(Love)

RAHAMIM
(Compassion)

HOD
(Majesty)

NETZAH
(Lasting
endurance)

YESOD
(Foundation of the world)

MALCHUT
(Kingdom)
or
SHECHINAH
(Indwelling)

DIVINE INTELLECT

MORAL QUALITIES

MATERIAL WORLD

INDWELLING PRESENCE

The first three Sefirot represent the processes of Divine thought: they are KETER ELYON (Supreme Crown – the Will of God, and the primary urge towards manifestation), which lead to the active HOCHMA (Wisdom) and to the passive BINAH (Understanding or Intellect). The next three Sefirot can be described as the moral attributes, with HESED (Love or Mercy) tempered by DIN (Strict Judgment, or Power), together leading to RAHAMIM (Compassion). The material world is represented by the active NETSAH (God's Lasting Endurance) and the passive HOD (God's Majesty), combining to produce YESOD (the Foundation of the World). The last Sefirah, MALCHUT (Kingdom), is God's indwelling presence in the world, and is often known as the SHECHINAH (Indwelling). The union of the higher Sefirot (flowing through Yesod) and Malchut is illustrated with specifically sexual symbolism in Kabbalah, whose masters write of the mystical union of the Holy One (blessed be He) with his Shechinah.

One of the most frequent representations of the Sefirot in literature is by means of the Tree of Divine Power. The masculine attributes are on the right, the feminine attributes are on the left, and those representing stability occupy the center. En-Sof is the hidden root of the tree, and is also the life-giving sap that travels up and down its branches. In another representation, the Sefirot are visualized as parts of a spiritual manifestation of the Divine in human form, known as Adam Kadmon (Primordial or Divine Man). When the Bible teaches that man was made in the image of God, the Zohar would have it that man was created in the image of a particular Divine manifestation, Adam Kadmon.

The Zohar

It is not necessary to be able to follow all the complex details of the system represented by the Sefirot to grasp the basic importance of its effect on religious thought and action. The Zohar states unequivocally that events and actions in one world must have their effects in the other worlds. Consequently the actions of each individual man, as well as those of the community of Israel, also have their influence in the Divine sphere. Man is thus placed squarely on the cosmic stage, with a vital role to play in the Divine drama that commenced with Adam's sin and expulsion. In the beginning, the Shechinah was present in the created world; and the unity and harmony of all existence was perfect, with the Divine power pulsing to and fro without interruption from En-Sof through the world of the Sefirot to the lower world of creation. Adam sinned; and as a result the Divine harmony was shattered, and the intimate connection of God to his creation was disturbed. Or, as the Zohar would express it, the Shechinah departed from the lower world and went into exile (mirrored by the exile of Israel from its Holy Land); and the union of the Holy One (blessed be He) with his Shechinah was disrupted. Man's primary task in this world is to exercise his God-given free will to heal that mystical flaw in the Divine pattern. This mission is called TIKKUN (restoration), which can be accomplished by the study of the Torah and the carrying out of its requirements, as well as by concentrated prayer and deep devotion to God. Only in this way can the world be redeemed and the true unity of God be restored.

Evil

The Kabbalah includes several different theories concerning the nature of evil. Most of these accept the existence of separate power of evil, somehow woven into the fabric of creation. One of the most interesting of the theories contained in the Zohar is based on the original perfect harmony of the Sefirot before the breach, when Strict Judgment (the Power or the Wrath of God) was always balanced by Love – these Sefirot acting together in differing proportions, one modified to some extent by the other. When this harmony was disturbed, God's Wrath was able to rage unabated by his Love; and part broke away from the world of the Sefirot to become the source of the evil we experience.

The Soul

Like many other ideas of the Kabbalah, those concerning the human soul are sometimes paradoxical. The Zohar teaches that the soul has three distinct parts:

NEFESH (life, or vitality), connected to the three lower Sefirot of the material world.

RUAH (spirit), connected to the three moral Sefirot.

NESHAMAH (higher soul), connected to the Sefirot of Divine Thought, and in particular to Binah (Intellect).

In the Nefesh, with which every man is endowed, the other elements are latent; and can be wakened by study, prayer and righteous acts. Neshamah, corresponding to Binah (God's Intellect) is the highest element of the three, and is of course the hardest to gain. The author of the Zohar believed in the rabbinic tradition that all souls were formed at creation, and also that they pre-existed in the world of the Sefirot. After death the soul separates into its constituent parts, each of which then returns to its original place in the Divine pattern: the lowest part, Nefesh, is first purified from sin by punishment. The Zohar fully accepts the idea of GILGUL (transmigration of souls), in which the souls of those who fail to perform certain duties in their lifetimes can be returned to earth after death, in another human form, for another chance.

Lurianic Kabbalah

The general teachings of Spanish Kabbalah, as portrayed in the Zohar and developed further in Safed, were given fresh direction by Isaac Luria, the 'Holy Lion'. Luria's ideas are complex and profound. They are not easy to describe briefly, and it would take many pages of explanation to do justice to their outlines, and to illustrate their fascinating implications.

According to the teachings of Isaac Luria, the drama of creation can be visualized in several distinct stages. At first the hidden, unknown and unknowable God (En-Sof) was all. Nothing existed or could exist outside God. Then God began a process of voluntary self-limitation or contraction. He withdrew himself into himself to leave a space that was without God. The space was not quite empty though, for it contained residual waste-products of the creative process – pictured as evil "husks" or "shells".

In the next stage, God (En-Sof) expanded his power by projecting manifestations of himself into the primeval void. This was the primary act of creation from which the world as we know it ultimately derives. Only those projected aspects of the hidden Divine Essence are accessible to human intellect. That, and only that, is what we call "God".

The Kabbalists saw the alternate limitation and projection, the contraction and expansion of divine power, as a continuing process needed to sustain creation – rather as the breathing in and out of air through the lungs is necessary to sustain the life of a human being. The original perfect harmony of God and his creation can be compared to that of a great tree, with its sap (Divine Power) pulsing steadily from its hidden root (the unknown Divine Essence) through its trunk (God's Manifestation in the World) to its outermost branches (Creation).

That ideal state was disturbed by an event described in the imagery of the Kabbalah as "the breaking of the vessels". This difficult concept can be pictured by imagining that God's projection of his manifestations into the primeval void was in the form of streams of particles of divine light, caught and stored in special containers. Some of the vessels burst, scattering the holy sparks far and wide among the evil husks that still littered the void. Luria explained that the breaking of the vessels was like an organic process, compared to the pod of a plant bursting to release its ripened seed. But it later came to be viewed as a cosmic catastrophe, a fundamental flaw in the act of creation – and it is this view that prevailed. As a result, divine power could no longer flow to and fro without interruption. The aspect of God known as the Shechinah (God's indwelling presence in the world) was separated from creation, and went into exile. Thus not only was the harmony of God's creation shattered, but so also was the essential unity of God in his own manifestations.

Kabbalah teaches that it is the duty of man to seek out the fallen holy sparks from the midst of the evil husks and restore them to their source; for only in that way can the primeval flaw be repaired and the harmony of God in his creation be made perfect once again. The message of Kabbalah was deeply satisfying. The Jews' own exile, exactly mirroring the exile of God from the world, suddenly took on profound meaning. No longer was the Jew a helpless spectator of the divine drama, passively waiting for the Messiah to redeem him. He now occupied a central position on the cosmic stage, with a crucial part to play in the redemption of Israel, of the world, and even of God himself. Only by his actions, consisting of concentrated prayer and meticulous observance of

God's commandments, could the breach be healed and true unity be restored.

The power of mystical prayer is given great emphasis in Lurianic Kabbalah, and is directed towards the great aim of 'Uniting the Holy One (blessed be He) with His Shechinah'. The sheer audacity of this concept, and of Luria's other doctrines, is quite staggering, though typical of the forms of religious thought expounded by the followers of the mystical tradition.

The universally accepted range of belief concerning Tikkun ensured that followers of the Kabbalah were always numbered amongst the most observant of their brethren, meticulously carrying out all the commandments of the Torah as interpreted by mainstream rabbinic tradition. Indeed their faith in the underlying mystical value of the least Mitzvah (commandment, or duty) encouraged them to perform the regular religious duties encumbent on all Jews with peculiar intensity and devotion.

Conclusion

In conclusion readers are warned not to be misled by the deceptive simplicity of the preceding paragraphs, by modern books on Kabbalah, or by English translations of Kabbalistic texts. Judgments should not be based on the descriptions contained in them. It cannot be emphasized too strongly that Kabbalistic doctrine is complex and obscure, and that it is expressed in strange allegorical terms. To those who know nothing of Judaism's mystical core the descriptions given above should be of some use in conveying a crude first impression of some of the ideas developed by its masters; but it must be remembered that they were written only for that very limited purpose.

IMPORTANCE

The wave of rationalism that overtook Judaism in the nineteenth century, and which is only just beginning to recede, ensured a consistent undervaluation and denigration of Kabbalah and its contribution to religious life. This tendency was reinforced by the deep-seated and long-lasting revulsion that followed the excesses of Shabbetai Zvi and his followers, and the subsequent low profile adopted by those who acknowledged the mystical tradition. However it must not be forgotten that large numbers of the most prominent of the sages and rabbis, famous for their contributions to rabbinic Judaism in its most formative periods, were also followers of the Kabbalah. Nachmanides is one of the very many names that immediately spring to mind in this connection, also Joseph Caro (author of the SHULHAN ARUCH, the definitive codification of Jewish law). It may surprise some readers to learn that the leading opponent of the East European Hasidic movement, the great Vilna Gaon himself, was also a lifelong master of Kabbalah. The mystical strand still runs deep in Judaism; and those unable to accept the reasoned approach to the fundamental problems of existence continue to be drawn to many of the ideas and methods implicit in the Kabbalah.

Part III

The Framework of Observance

8

The Jewish Year

THE CALENDAR

There are significant differences between the Jewish calendar employed for all religious purposes, and the secular calendar in general use. As the workings of any calendar are simply taken for granted by most people, an account of its origins may be of interest.

Two of the three most natural periods into which time can be divided – the day and the year – are governed by the movement of the earth relative to the sun: the third is governed by the moon. Primitive man was almost completely dependent on the growing of food crops; and it was soon realized that the orderly succession of seasons in which seeds are sown, crops grow, ripen and are harvested, correspond exactly to various positions of the sun in the sky. The sun was worshipped as the sustainer of life in most early civilizations; and the passage of time very naturally came to be measured in solar 'years' related to the cycle of the sun's movement through the heavens.

The moon was also worshipped in the ancient world: the regular waxing and waning of its disc could easily be seen by all, and was thought to be crucial for the renewal of life on earth. Therefore the moon's cycle, the lunar 'month', also came to be used to measure the passing of time. Unfortunately for the makers of calendars, the earth's revolution round the sun takes just over 365 days, while the moon circles the earth in just over 29½ days. Hence a period of twelve lunar months falls short of a solar year by about eleven days; and the two cannot easily be reconciled. As the agricultural rhythm was of such primary importance, most calendars had to be constructed so as to ensure that main events, such as the harvest, always took place at the same time of year – otherwise the seasons would drift from month to month with the passing of the years.

The Jews, like many other early peoples, adopted a calendar based partly on the moon and partly on the sun. They carefully watched the sky for the new moon, and marked the beginning of each lunar month by the reappearance of its crescent. They also attempted to regulate the length of the year by the movements of the sun. As twelve lunar months is about eleven days short of a solar year, constant corrections had to be made to the calendar to ensure that the agricultural festivals always occurred in the same season. For example, Passover (in the Hebrew month of Nissan) marks the end of the winter rains in Israel, and must always be celebrated on a full moon in early spring. A luni-solar calendar of this kind is very complex, as it has to satisfy technical astronomical criteria as well as religious and agricultural needs.

The modern Jewish calendar was developed from earlier models, and reached its present form in the tenth century c.e. Time is divided into cycles of nineteen years, with a leap year in each 3rd, 6th, 8th, 11th, 14th, 17th and 19th year of a cycle. Ordinary years contain twelve lunar months; and leap years contain thirteen lunar months.

In contrast, the modern secular calendar is based only on the solar year. Its calendar year contains 365 days, with an extra day added in every fourth year (leap year). The use of the lunar month has been abandoned; and the year is divided artificially into twelve calendar months, seven of 31 days, four of 30 days and one of 28 days (or 29 days in a leap year).

The Jewish day starts and ends at sunset, corresponding to the account of the phasing of the days of creation in the Book of Genesis: 'So evening came, and morning came, the first day.'

Between the day and the lunar month, other intermediate but artificial periods of time also came into use in past ages. These so-called weeks varied in length between five and ten days in different societies, and usually marked the interval between successive market days. The Israelites, firmly believing that God had created the world in six days and that he had rested on the seventh, divided their days into weeks of seven days each. This division has since become standard throughout the world.

In biblical times individual years were identified by reference to the reign of a particular ruler – for example, a man might say that he had been born in the third year of the reign of King David. Other fixed reference points, such as the destruction of the Temple, came into use later. From time to time rabbis and scholars attempted to compute the age of the earth from information obtained from the Bible, literally interpreted. Final agreement was reached in the thirteenth century C.E. that the year of creation was 3761 B.C.E. From that time on, Jewish years have been numbered from that agreed date – for example, 1 October 1980 corresponds to the Jewish date 21 Tishri 5741 A.M. (anno mundi, or year since creation).

THE SABBATH

Thus the heavens and the earth was finished with all their mighty host. And on the seventh day God ended His work which He had made; and He rested on the seventh day from all His work which He had made. And God blessed the seventh day and sanctified it. . . .[1]

The description of creation in the Book of Genesis is remarkably succinct, considering its subject. Though in the light of scientific knowledge modern apologists may interpret the biblical time span of 'seven days' in a rather different manner, the ancient Israelites accepted it literally. When the Jews were commanded to imitate the ways of their Creator by perpetually observing the sanctity of each seventh day – the Sabbath – as 'a memorial of the work of creation', this became one of the most important and distinctive marks of their faith.

Remember the Sabbath day to keep it holy. Six days shall you labor and do all your work. But the seventh day is the Sabbath of the Lord your God: in it you shall do no work, you, nor your son, nor your daughter, your manservant, nor your maidservant, your cattle, nor any stranger who is within your gates.[2]

It would be hard to exaggerate the importance of the Sabbath in traditional Judaism. Observance of the Sabbath is listed directly after statements dealing with belief in God in the Ten commandments. The command to honor the Sabbath day, to keep it holy and to refrain work on it, is no peripheral injunction to the observant Jew. It is a pivot on which the organization of his life turns. The Rabbis teach that of all institutions it is the Sabbath that has done most to preserve the Jewish faith and people throughout their long history. The Jewish idea of dividing time into periods of seven days, with a compulsory rest day in each period, has by now also been adopted by the rest of mankind, to their benefit. However, for reasons of their own, the 'daughter' faiths of Christianity and Islam observe the day of rest on a day other than the seventh.

And it was evening, and it was morning, the sixth day.[3]

The Sabbath commences one hour before sunset each Friday evening. Its onset is greeted with joy by the faithful, who compare its coming to that of a bride (the Sabbath) approaching her bridegroom (the Jewish people). The home is the focus of celebration. Before the evening meal two festive candles are lit, and God is blessed over wine in the KIDDUSH (sanctification) for having caused Israel, in love, to inherit the Sabbath as a memorial of the work of creation, and also as a memorial of the deliverance of the Jewish people from slavery in Egypt. Three special meals are consumed on the Sabbath. Passages from the Torah (Five Books of Moses – Genesis, Exodus, Leviticus, Numbers and Deuteronomy) are publicly recited in the synagogues, followed by selected passages from the Prophets. People greet each other with the salutation SHABBAT SHALOM (Shalom meaning peace), or with the homely Anglo-Yiddish 'Good Shabbos'. At sunset on Saturday evening the ceremony of HAVDALAH (distinction, i.e. between the Sabbath and ordinary days) marks the end of the Sabbath; and the pangs of its departure are lessened by the taste of wine and the scent of fragrant spices.

The Divine order to refrain from work on the Sabbath has been the subject of much detailed interpretation and legislation by the Rabbis. Since God ceased to create on the seventh day, all actions which are considered to be of a creative nature are forbidden to the Jew, in order to remind him of his dependence on the Creator. Apart from what is ordinarily understood by work many other things are forbidden, such as carrying any object beyond the home, walking for more than a specified distance outside a built-up area, handling money, writing, and making fire. As sparks can be caused by activating electrical appliances, the observant Jew will not switch on a light, television set or cooker on the Sabbath, nor will he ride in a car or bus. Of course ways are found to mitigate the severity of these ordinances without transgressing. For example, electric time-switches set before the Sabbath can be used to good effect, and food can be kept cooking very slowly throughout the day.

Sabbath laws may be neglected only for the purpose of preserving or saving human life, in which case it becomes a positive duty to break them.

Proper observance of the Sabbath is often very difficult to achieve in a secular society. For example, the early setting of the sun on a Friday afternoon in mid-winter will mean that the pious Jew will have to leave work shortly after lunch in order to reach home in time. Though rabbinic interpretation of Sabbath work prohibitions may seem draconian, by forcing the observant Jew to break his daily routine in this way the Rabbis have provided a framework with which to add a spiritual dimension to life. To those who keep it, the Sabbath is a day of tranquility and joy when all worries and worldly thoughts are left behind.

THE NEW MOON

ROSH HODESH (head of the month) marks the start of each new month in the Jewish calendar. It was celebrated as a minor festival in former times, when a special sacrifice was offered in the Temple.

Only vestiges of the former significance of the New Moon survive today, when its advent is solemnly announced in the synagogues. If the New Moon falls on the Sabbath, portions are read from two Sefarim (scrolls of the Law) instead of from the usual one. Special psalms of rejoicing (the Hallel) are recited on the day of the New Moon.

Before the timing of the New Moon came to be determined by calculation, a special court assembled in Jerusalem on the thirtieth day of each month for that purpose. As soon as two reliable witnesses testified to the reappearance of the crescent moon in the sky, the New Moon was proclaimed and a beacon lit on the Mount of Olives. Signals and messages were then transmitted to all parts of Israel. If the moon's crescent was not seen on the thirtieth of the month, the New Moon was celebrated on the following day. Jews from beyond the borders of Israel observed the New Moon on the thirtieth day of each month, and again on the thirty-first, to make quite sure that they did not miss the right day. This doubt led to the custom outside Israel of celebrating all holy days in the calendar (except for the Day of Atonement) on two successive days; and like much else in Jewish practice, this duplication continues commemoratively, even though its original purpose has long since disappeared. In Israel (and in Reform Temples) only one day is observed, other than for Rosh Hashana.

MAJOR FESTIVALS

Three times a year all your males shall come into the presence of the Lord your God in the place which He will choose; at the pilgrim feasts of Unleavened Bread, of Weeks and of Tabernacles. . . .[4]

The three great pilgrim festivals each have a double significance. They have aspects which relate them closely to events in the agricultural year; and they are also intimately connected to the earliest events in the history of the Jewish people. In post-biblical times, these historic events became dominant – at Passover (or the feast of Unleavened Bread) the birth of the nation is celebrated: Shavuot (the feast of Weeks, or Pentecost) marks the encounter with God at Mount Sinai; and during Succot (Tabernacles) Jews remember the time that their ancestors spent in the wilderness, travelling between Egypt and their Promised Land.

As there are a large number of excellent books readily

available on the subject of Jewish holy days, only an outline of their salient features is included here.

Pesah (Passover)

You shall keep this day as a day of remembrance . . . for all time.[5]

Passover, or the feast of Unleavened Bread, is an eight-day long celebration of the deliverance of the Hebrews from slavery in Egypt.

The Lord brought us out of Egypt with a mighty hand and with an outstretched arm, with great terribleness and with signs and wonders.[6]

And the Lord brought us forth from Egypt, not by means of an angel, or a seraph, or a messenger – but by the Holy One, blessed be He, Himself in His glory. . . .[7]

Even though this is where the towering figure of Moses first appears in Jewish history, great stress is laid throughout the festival on God's own personal role in the redemption.

'For seven days you shall eat unleavened bread . . . anyone who eats leavened bread shall be outlawed from Israel.'[8] In obedience to the biblical command, all bread and other fermented products are scrupulously removed from the home before the start of the festival – this extends to kitchen utensils and to crockery that has been in contact with leaven during the year. The consumption of all such food is forbidden during Passover, to remind Jews that their ancestors were hurried out of Egypt.

. . . and the people picked up their dough before it was leavened. . . .[9]

The dough that they had brought from Egypt was baked into unleavened cakes, because there was no leaven; for they had been driven out of Egypt and allowed no time even to get food ready for themselves.[10]

The festival starts in the home with a special ceremonial dinner called the SEDER (order, or arrangement) – the 'last supper' of the New Testament. The youngest person present asks: 'Why is this night different from all other nights?' and the answer to that question forms the basis of the narrative which follows. The descendants (actual, or spiritual) of the slaves remember the time of oppression and lovingly recount the traditional story of the events which led to freedom – while leaning back in their chairs, drinking wine and feasting. Unfortunately, human oppression did not end with the exodus from Egypt. Grievous circumstances, now and in the past, serve constantly to keep fresh the message of Passover, the festival of freedom.

Passover is observed at a full moon in early spring, and marks the transition from winter to summer. Prayers for dew, to 'slake the scorching earth', are included in the synagogue service for the first day of the festival:

> May the trees be full of sap . . . the threshing floors filled with corn, and the vats overflow with wine and oil . . . and may the heavens give their dews.[11]

In Israel the first and seventh days are full holidays; and the intermediate days, when normal work is permitted, are of lesser importance. Outside Israel, because of original doubts concerning the actual day of the full moon, the first two days and the seventh and eighth days are observed as full holidays.

Shavuot (Weeks)

> . . . I have carried you on eagles' wings and brought you here to Me. If only you will now listen to Me and keep My covenant, then . . . you shall be My kingdom of priests, My holy nation.[12]

The act of gaining freedom from slavery was not enough to forge a nation. So seven weeks after Passover, Jews celebrate the supreme event in their history, when, in the desert of Sinai, they received the Torah (teaching) from God.

There were peals of thunder and flashes of lightning, dense cloud on the mountain and a loud trumpet blast: the people in the camp were all terrified.[13]

By their act of accepting God's Law at Sinai, the Hebrew tribes acquired a reason for their freedom, a stamp of nationhood to which they have clung with remarkable tenacity ever since. And each year Jews strive anew to be a chosen people, and not merely a chosen one.

There never arose in Israel a prophet who, like Moses, did behold the likeness of God.[14]

Moses, venerated above all other men in Jewish tradition, played a key role in the events commemorated at Shavuot. However this is the festival which celebrates the giving of the Torah at Sinai. It is concerned primarily with the central relationship of the Jewish nation to its God, compared to which the significance of individual people and places is unimportant. For example, Moses – who negotiated with Pharoah for the freedom of his people, who led them through the desert to the boundary of the Promised Land, and who received the Ten Commandments and the Torah on their behalf – has no shrine. His place of burial remains unknown; and no festival, not even Shavuot, is consecrated to his memory. Also, Mount Sinai, the dramatic setting for the act of revelation, is no longer regarded by Jews as a holy place. The late (Egyptian) President Sadat's suggestion of building a synagogue, together with a mosque and a church, on the summit of its supposed site was received with indifference in Israel.

In the time of the Temple the first ripe fruits of the season were brought to the sanctuary at Shavuot, which marked the end of the barley harvest and the beginning of the wheat harvest. Today, synagogues are decorated with flowers and plants for the festival. The central point of the service is the reading from the Torah of the account of the events at Sinai, when all stand for the recital of the Ten Commandments. The Book of Ruth, a harvest story, is also read. A charming old practice, still observed in Gibraltar and elsewhere, is the reading of a KETUBAH (formal marriage contract) in the synagogue to symbolize the 'marriage' of the Jewish people to the Torah.

It is customary to eat dairy products in the home during the festival, for the Torah is compared to milk: 'Your lips drop sweetness like the honeycomb, my bride. Syrup and milk are under your tongue.'[15]

The first night of Shavuot is observed by the devout as an all-night vigil, spent in reading the Torah and other religious works.

Succot (Tabernacles)

> You shall live in booths (tabernacles) for seven days . . . so that your descendants may be reminded how I made the Israelites live in booths when I brought them out of Egypt.[16]

This has become the prime significance of the festival of Succot, when Jews erect temporary huts (SUCCOT) and dwell in them for the seven days of the holiday. The SUKKAH (booth: singular) must be built in the open: it is roofed with branches, leaves or straw, and left partly open to the sky. In cold or wet climates people rarely sleep in the Sukkah, but they do eat their meals there, weather permitting.

> On the fifteenth day of the seventh month, when the harvest has been gathered, you shall keep the Lord's pilgrim feast for seven days . . . you shall take the fruit of the citrus tree, palm fronds, leafy branches, and willows from the riverside, and you shall rejoice before the Lord your God. . . .[17]

Succot is also a harvest festival, celebrating the 'ingathering from the threshing floor and from the winepress', and the Sukkah is lavishly decorated with hangings of fruit and vegetables. The palm frond is bound together with the other specified leafy branches into a garland, called a LULAV: this, with an ETROG (large and fragrant citrus fruit) is held in the hand and shaken by worshippers during the recital of the Hallel psalms (nos. 113 to 118) of rejoicing in the synagogue. The Lulav and Etrog are also carried in solemn procession round a Sefer Torah (Scroll of the Law), stationed on the Bimah (platform containing the reading desk), as they were carried round the altar of the Temple in former times. On

HOSHANA RABBA, the seventh day of Succot, the procession goes round the Bimah seven times to the accompaniment of HOSHANA (Save us) prayers for the success of the harvest and other enterprises in the coming year.

The first day (and the second day outside Israel) are full holy days on which no work is allowed, also the eighth day, called SHEMINI AZERET (eighth day of solemn assembly) on which prayers for rain are recited in the synagogue. The last day of the festival is SIMHAT TORAH (Rejoicing of the Law) and marks the end of the yearly series of readings during which the entire Five Books of Moses are recited in the synagogue. The person called to the reading of the last portion of the Book of Deuteronomy is known as the HATAN TORAH (Bridegroom of the Torah). The person called to the reading of the first portion of the Book of Genesis, the start of the new cycle, is known as the HATAN B'RAYSHIT (Bridegroom of Genesis: B'rayshit is the first word in the Book of Genesis, the first book of the Bible). All the scrolls are carried in procession round the synagogue. In the service for the eve of Simhat Torah, there is much celebration, and men will often dance with a Sefer Torah in their arms.

DAYS OF AWE

. . . O Lord our God, impose Your awe on all Your works and Your dread upon all You have created, that all Your works may revere You and all Your creatures prostrate themselves before You, and all together do Your will with a perfect heart.[18]

The first ten days of the Hebrew month of Tishri, starting with the New Year (ROSH HASHANA) and ending with the Day of Atonement (YOM KIPPUR) are regarded as a particularly solemn period of the year. Rosh Hashana is a day of judgment in which, to quote the Rabbis, God opens the Book of Life and enters the deeds of each individual. On Yom Kippur, the Book of Life is sealed, finally. The season, known as the Ten Days of Penitence, is a time of self-examination and of imploring God's pardon for transgressions against Divine law.

Rosh Hashana (Head of the Year)

The Jewish New Year, celebrated at the new moon of the Hebrew month of Tishri, and on the following day, is also known as the Day of Judgment, the Day of Memorial, and the Day of the Blowing of the Shofar.

A trumpet, made from the horn of a ram (Shofar), is blown repeatedly during part of the synagogue service. Its sound is intended to instil feelings of awe in the minds of the worshippers; and according to Sa'adya Gaon:

1. As a memorial of the day of creation, when God assumed Kingship over the world – the triumphant sound of coronation.

2. As a warning to repent from evil ways, on this first of the Ten Penitential Days.

3. As a reminder of the giving of the Torah on Mount Sinai, when 'the sound of the SHOFAR waxed exceeding loud'.

4. As a reminder of the warnings of the Prophets – compared to blasts on the trumpet.

5. As a reminder of the destruction of the Temple – a sound of warfare.

6. As a reminder of the willingness of Isaac to be bound as a sacrifice to God, and of God's mercy – a ram was sacrificed instead.

7. To make its hearers 'tremble and quake with fear', so that they may humble themselves before God.

8. As a reminder of the great Day of Judgment to come, which will be proclaimed by the sound of the Shofar.

9. As a reminder of the messianic age to come, when the outcasts of Israel will return to worship in Jerusalem to the sound of the Shofar.

10. As a reminder of the resurrection of the dead, when the Shofar will be sounded.

Rosh Hashana is not a simple celebration of the new year, but rather a day of special solemnity. People greet each other with the hope that they may be inscribed in the Book of Life for the coming year, or that they may be granted 'many years' to come. In the ceremonial meal on the eve it is customary to eat sweet apple dipped in honey, and to pray, 'Renew unto us a good and sweet year'. Sephardim have a more elaborate ritual, displaying and eating other foods of symbolic significance.

Day of Atonement (Kippur)

Yom Kippur, as it is popularly known, is the last of the Ten Days of Penitence. It is the most solemn day of the year, a day of affliction in which Jews fast (no food or drink) from an hour before sunset on one day to shortly after sunset on the following day, a time of complete abstention from normal activity - a Sabbath of Sabbaths - devoted entirely to introspection and prayer.

In the day-long succession of synagogue services, worshippers are made conscious of human inadequacy and sinfulness. Humbled in spirit and afflicted by self-imposed deprivation, they confess their shortcomings to God, and seek forgiveness. A central part of the services is the detailed description of former proceedings in the Temple, when the High Priest sacrificed to make atonement for the people, and the scapegoat carrying their sins was driven out of the city and killed: all bow low when the Divine Name is referred to in the recital, for God's presence is felt to be close.

In the last service of the day – the NE'ILA, the symbolic closing of the gates of heaven – members of the congregation throw themselves more confidently on God's mercy: 'The Lord is near those . . . who call upon Him in truth . . . He will hear their cry, and will save them';[19] and pray that they may 'enter Your gates'.

The service concludes with a triumphant blast on the Shofar, proclaiming the new freedom gained by self-imposed afflictions, prayer and Divine grace. The day which began with bodily mortification ends with spiritual exaltation: 'Go, eat your bread with joy, and drink your wine with a glad heart; for the Lord has already accepted your works.'[20]

Something must be added here concerning two popular misconceptions regarding the cancelling of vows and the forgiveness of sins on Yom Kippur. In the first service of Yom Kippur, KAL NIDRE (all vows), all promises and vows made by man to his Creator are annulled: this does not apply to obligations between man and man. Forgiveness of sins is a matter of Divine grace that can occur only if there is genuine repentance expressed by remorse for the sinful act, a determination to desist from repetition, and positive attempts to make amends and to do good. The Talmud states that the Day of Atonement will not bring pardon if a man says 'I will sin, and Yom Kippur will bring pardon'. If one individual has wronged another during the year it is customary for appropriate amends and apologies to be made on or before Yom Kippur as part of the same process.

MINOR FESTIVALS AND FASTS

Purim

This festival is marked by the reading of the Book of Esther in the synagogue. It commemorates the deliverance of the Jews of the Persian Empire from the evil designs of Haman, vizier to King Ahasuerus (possibly the historic King Xerxes 486–465 B.C.E.). A carnival atmosphere prevails at Purim.

Hanuka (Dedication)

An eight-branched candlestick or oil lamp is used to celebrate the rededication of the Temple after the victory of Judas Maccabeus over the Syrian Greeks in 165 B.C.E. One light is lit on the first night of the festival, two on the second night, and so on until all shine together on the last night.

Tu Bi-Shevat

TU BI-SHEVAT (15th of the month of Shevat) is the New Year of Trees.

Lag Ba'Omer

LAG BA'OMER is in honor of the great mystic and patriot Shimon Bar Yochai. It interrupts the period of semi-mourning between Passover and Shavuot during which marriages are not performed in memory of the death from plague of the disciples of Rabbi Akivah.

Yom Ha-Azmaut

YOM HA-AZMAUT (Independence Day) celebrates the birth of the modern State of Israel in 1948. Thanksgiving services are held in many synagogues.

Yom Yerushalayim

YOM YERUSHALAYIM (Day of Jerusalem) is the most recent festive day in the calendar. It commemorates the recapture of Jerusalem in 1967, following a period of almost twenty years when Jews were denied all access to the Holy City, and during which their synagogues and cemetery were desecrated.

Tisha Be'Av (9th day of the month of Av)

This important fast commemorates the destruction of the first Temple in 586 B.C.E. and of the second Temple in 70 C.E. Synagogues are often draped in black on the day of the fast, and special lamentations are recited.

No marriages are performed during the three weeks that precede Tisha Be'Av; and the nine days before the fast are observed as a period of semi-mourning.

Other Fasts

17th Tammuz commemorates the breaching of the walls of Jerusalem in the first and second Temple periods.

10th Tevet marks the siege of Jerusalem by Nebuchadnezzar, King of Babylon in 588 B.C.E.

The fast of Gedaliah is in memory of the assassination of Gedaliah, governor of the kingdom of Judah, in 586 B.C.E.

The fast of Esther is observed one day before Purim.

The fast of the Firstborn is observed on the day before Passover.

9

The Home

DAILY LIFE

For the observant Jew the practice of his faith is not confined to the synagogue. There is no boundary between religion and everyday life; and both are inextricably intertwined. Between reciting one prayer on waking in the morning and another before falling asleep at night, he will try to carry out as many as possible of the seventy-seven positive obligations that the Rabbis teach are now presently capable of fulfillment (from the original six hundred and thirteen positive and negative precepts formulated when the Temple still stood). Thus numerous daily actions, otherwise trivial in themselves, are invested with a spiritual dimension.

Of course observance of this intensity carries with it a very real risk of degenerating into mere routine, performed for its own sake; and the Rabbis constantly warn against this danger. At its best though, it forms the basis for a way of living that is permeated with awareness of the abiding wonder of creation. Most Jews adopt some compromise between the extremes of complete indifference and full piety, accepting as much or as little of the ritual that is personally meaningful.

For the more traditional, it is the home rather than the synagogue, that is the true center of religious observance. Consequently, Jewish home life is noted for its warmth and for the mutual supportiveness of its members, young and old alike.

PRAYER

A short prayer is pronounced on waking in the morning:

I give thanks to You, O King, who lives and endures, for in mercy You have restored my soul to me: great is Your faithfulness.

On rising from bed, the hands are washed and the following blessing is recited: 'Blessed are You O Lord our God, King of the universe, who has commanded us to wash the hands.'

The traditional small fringed garment (TZIZIT), worn constantly by men under their normal clothes, is then put on to the accompaniment of another benediction.

When the statutory morning, afternoon and evening services are said at home and not in the synagogue, they follow the same basic form, except that those parts requiring a Minyan (quorum of at least ten adult males) are omitted – mainly the reading from the Torah, and prayers such as the Kaddish. Tefillin are worn by men for morning prayers, except on Sabbaths and holy days. The reader should refer to chapter ten for details of the services and principal prayers; to chapter two, 'Bar Mitzvah' for a description of Tefillin; and to the section on the Shema, one of the principal prayers, for the origin of the fringed garment.

There is a ritual washing of the hands before each meal, accompanied by the blessing. A short benediction is pronounced over bread. Any meal that includes bread, the original staple food, is followed by a long Grace After Meals in which God is thanked for having provided. It also includes prayers to cover many other needs as well:

. . . O Lord our God have mercy on us and on Your people Israel, and on Your city of Jerusalem, and on Mount Zion the place of Your glory . . . feed us, sustain us, provide for us . . . relieve us from all our anxieties. . . .[1]

Many of the little incidents of everyday living are also marked by the recitation of special blessings. A large number of these exist, ranging from the one said after the evacuation of the bowels, to others uttered when seeing trees in blossom, sighting a rainbow, a king, or a distinguished rabbi. The list is long.

As a man's head must be covered when praying, it will be appreciated that the constant wearing of a KIPPAH (skull cap) makes sense. It is also worn as a symbol of religious awareness, a visible sign of respect to the Almighty.

THE FAMILY

Family life, centered in the home, is fundamental to Jewish tradition, which teaches that a human being is incomplete until married. A full sex life within marriage is also considered essential, abstinence being a prime ground for divorce.

God's commandment to man to 'be fruitful and multiply' is observed in its literal sense, at the very least until one son and one daughter have been born to the marriage. Children are greatly prized, and their education is a primary religious duty.

Ceremonies involving the whole family – such as the Kiddush (sanctification) on Friday nights and festivals, and the Passover Seder – help to generate strong emotional ties, which often endure even among those who have ceased to observe these customs in their own lives. Such feelings are further strengthened by the mourning rites carried out in the home following a death in the family, and by the joyful celebration of marriage, Bar Mitzvah, Bat Mitzvah, and birth.

Part I on 'The Ages of Man' deals in detail with the laws and customs of birth, religious majority, marriage, death and mourning. The reader is referred to chapter eight for an account of many of the home ceremonies.

The current breakdown of established discipline and morality is taking its toll of Jewish families, just as it is in most other sections of modern society. One possible explanation is that people have not yet learned how to use their newly achieved freedoms properly. Another is that adults, like children, function best within a generally accepted framework of restraint, whether religious, moral, or merely social. It is true that traditional Jewish family life may have its drawbacks as well as its virtues. It can, for example, sometimes stifle its younger members, almost inciting them to rebel from its benevolent tyranny. But on the positive side, it provides a stable and secure background from which an individual can emerge with a sound sense of values, and with sufficient confidence to maintain it in the face of the moral anarchy that can so often engulf the unprepared.

DIETARY LAWS (Kashrut)

These fall into three main parts – permitted and forbidden foods, the preparation of meat for consumption, and the separation of milk and meat. The laws are complicated; but a short summary of aspects that most affect observant Jews in English-speaking countries is given here.

I give you all plants that bear seed everywhere on earth, and every tree bearing fruit which yields seed.[2]

In compliance with the biblical statement, all fruit and vegetables may be eaten.

Animals which both chew the cud and have cloven hooves are permitted for food: all others are prohibited, including pig, rabbit and horse. Only fish that have both scales and fins (at least one of each) may be eaten: all others are forbidden, including sturgeon (caviar), eel, shark, and shellfish. Reptiles, insects and 'creeping things' are not allowed, including frogs. A list of permitted birds and fowl is included in the Bible: among others, all birds of prey are forbidden. Animals which have died of natural causes may not be eaten, nor may those suffering from disease.

You shall eat none of the blood, whether of bird or beast, wherever you may live. Any person who eats any of the blood shall be cut off from his father's kin.[3]

All animals intended for food must be killed in the specified manner, the process being known as SHEHITAH (ritual slaughter). This can only be done by a qualified man, the SHOHET, who has been highly trained in the minutiae of this facet of religious law. The instrument used is the knife, which must satisfy exacting standards of sharpness in order to minimize pain and cause almost instantaneous unconsciousness. The throat is cut; and as much blood as possible drained from the carcass, which is then examined carefully for any defects or injuries that would render the meat unfit for use. Abdominal fat is removed, as this was once sacrificed on the altar. In memory of Jacobs's struggle with the angel, the sciatic nerve is also removed: 'Israelites to this day do not eat the sinew of the nerve that runs in the hollow of the thigh.'[4]

Shehitah is without doubt one of the most humane methods of slaughter available. However, since the development of modern methods of stunning beasts prior to killing, Shehitah sometimes comes under attack. A powerful lobby periodically attempts to have Shehitah banned on the grounds of cruelty; but Jews and their supporters continue to maintain stoutly that their method is still as humane as any other, and that it minimizes suffering. It is a difficult subject.

You shall not boil a kid in its mother's milk.[5]

This biblical command has been expanded by the Rabbis until it now involves the complete separation of all foods containing traces of any milk product (such as butter or cheese) from those containing meat. Food containing meat and food containing milk may not be eaten together at the same meal. Meat can be consumed soon after milk if the mouth is rinsed first, or bread eaten. Milk may not be eaten after meat before an interval of several hours, the precise period depending on local custom. As these two types of food are kept completely apart throughout all stages of storage, preparation, cooking and eating, most orthodox Jewish institutions and hotels maintain two separate kitchens, one for milk and the other for meat. Restaurants will usually be equipped to serve only one or the other.

Neutral food (PARVE), such as bread, eggs, vetetables and fruit, may be consumed either with milk or with meat.

For her home, the observant Jewish housewife will obtain all her meat and poultry from a Kosher butcher, who will only sell meat that has been slaughtered under strict rabbinic supervision. Most butchers will also 'kasher' the meat – that is removing all traces of blood from it by soaking it in cold water for half an hour, then sprinkling it with salt and allowing it to drain for a further hour before washing it again two or three times in cold water. If the butcher does not 'kasher' the meat, this must be done at home.

Complete separation of milk and meat in the kitchen must be ensured. Separate storage, washing facilities (two sinks), sets of cooking utensils, sets of crockery and cutlery must be provided for each type of food. The pans and dishes must be washed up and dried apart from each other. In essence the Jewish housewife runs two parallel kitchens in the space of one room. Though this sounds awkward, it is not nearly so difficult in practice where it simply becomes an accepted routine.

And why, a disinterested observer may ask, have Jews developed such awkward and elaborate laws to regulate their eating habits? Why must they afflict themselves with standards of observance so much higher even than those set out in the Bible, and from which most of them so often fall short? The Bible itself is fairly clear about the reason for its lists of permitted and forbidden foods, and its strictures on the drinking of blood: 'You shall be holy unto Me, therefore you shall not eat...'[6] and 'I have set you apart from the peoples that you shall be Mine.'[7] In other words certain rules of 'holiness' or 'apartness' are imposed on the Jewish people to enable it to become 'a light unto the nations', and to transmit the Divine message to all mankind.

The Rabbis, in their own words, made 'a fence round the Torah', and developed the original basic laws to the extent that the simple prohibition of boiling a kid in its mother's milk expanded into the elaborate rules described above. The Rabbis of the Talmudic era did not seem to have had many doubts concerning the primary purpose of Kashrut – it was to refine man by disciplining his basic appetites: '... what does the Holy One, blessed be He, care whether a man kills an animal by its throat or by the nape of its neck. Its purpose is to refine man himself.'[8]

In later ages all kinds of practical, pseudo-rational reasons for Kashrut were advanced. The most popular of these explanations is founded on the need to preserve man's health. For example, pigs can scavenge in filth (as they still do in India today) and carry disease: shellfish breed best in polluted water and are prone to contamination. This kind of reasoning alone can easily be refuted – the horse, to quote only one instance, has always been a 'clean' animal, but is forbidden nevertheless. The reader should assess for himself the weight of argument available on this topic.

When all has been said, it is the early reasons which still seem to have the most validity today. Dietary laws were introduced to set the people apart, to enable them better to fulfill their role of interpreters and teachers of God's law. The rules were then developed to give man an opportunity of disciplining his appetites above the level of the animal world, and to remind him constantly of a higher plane of existence.

10

The Synagogue

HISTORY

The synagogue as a house of assembly, study and prayer is one of the distinctly original Jewish contributions to world religion. With its liturgy, it has served as a direct model for both the church and the mosque.

The origins of the institution are lost in the distant past. Some scholars believe that synagogues existed at the time of King Solomon's Temple: others disagree. It is generally accepted that the synagogue was either started or considerably developed by the Jews deported to Babylon by King Nebuchadnezzar after his destruction of Jerusalem in the year 586 B.C.E. Under the direction of their prophets the exiles turned to the Torah for guidance, seeking a cure for their suffering and means for their future redemption. Lacking the Temple on which to concentrate their religious life, they assembled regularly in a BETH HA-KNESSET (house of assembly, or synagogue) to hear the Torah read and explained, and to offer prayers to God. It is easy to see how, in such circumstances, the synagogue developed as a place for prayer and study, as well as a social, cultural and commercial center for the exiles, far from home in a foreign land.

Not much is known about the next period in the history of the synagogue; but those who returned to the land of Israel from exile must have taken the institution back with them. By the first century C.E. the synagogue had become a vital part of contemporary Jewish life in Israel; and it is interesting to note that it was then regarded as an institution of great antiquity. According to the Talmud there were several hundred synagogues in Jerusalem by 70 C.E. We even have an account of a Day of Atonement service in a synagogue on

Temple Mount itself, with the High Priest reading from the Torah. The Temple, with its sacrificial rituals, was aptly complemented by the synagogue, with its emphasis on learning and communal prayer.

Outside the Holy Land synagogues flourished wherever Jews lived. Those familiar with the Christian scriptures will have read how the teachers of the new religion sought converts in synagogue after synagogue in most of the principal cities of the then civilized world. Though tradition ascribes the establishment of the Shef ve-Yatif synagogue (in Iraq) to the first Babylonian exiles, the earliest tangible evidence that we now possess of the existence of a particular synagogue is a marble slab uncovered in Egypt during the early years of this century. The inscription on that stone declares that the Shedia synagogue (near Alexandria) was dedicated to King Ptolemy III and his Queen, who reigned from 246 to 221 B.C.E. The Talmud contains a description of the Great Synagogue of Alexandria which was destroyed in about 100 C.E. So vast was this building that a system of flags had to be used there in order to prompt responses from the congregation, many of whom were seated so far away from the Reader that they were unable to hear him.

When the Temple existed it was the focus of religious feeling for the Jewish people, and their center of pilgrimage. Its impressive rituals were designed for the primary function of offering sacrifices to God. However prayers were also recited by the priests, with the central confession of Jewish faith – the Shema: 'Hear O Israel, the Lord is our God, the Lord is ONE...' – and the Ten Commandments being regularly proclaimed. The people were blessed by the priests with the formula from the Book of Numbers:

> May the Lord bless you and keep you.
> May the Lord cause His face to shine upon you and be gracious unto you.
> May the Lord look kindly on you and give you peace.[1]

Psalms were sung by the Levites (to the accompaniment of musical instruments), including the Hallel (praise) – Psalms 113 to 118 – on special days of thanksgiving and rejoicing. There is not much evidence of a place for communal prayer in the Temple service; and participation by the people seems to have been limited to standard responses such as 'Blessed be He; Blessed be His name'.

People assembled in the synagogues to hear the Torah read and explained on Sabbaths, as well as on Mondays and Thursdays which were market days. They also met in the synagogues for daily prayer sessions, timed to coincide with the regular sacrifices in the Temple. The principal prayer, called Tefillah (the Prayer) – or more familiarly known as the AMIDAH (standing), or the SHEMONEH-ESREH (Eighteen Benedictions) – is said to have originated in the time of Ezra (about 400 B.C.E.), though its form did not become standardised until after the destruction of the Temple. The Amidah was, and still remains, the main prayer of the liturgy; and its recital is obligatory for 'orthodox' Jews at each time of day that a sacrifice would have been offered in the Temple.

After the destruction of the Temple by the Romans in the year 70 C.E. the Rabbis worked long and hard to preserve the Jewish faith under conditions of defeat and oppression, and in the absence of the national shrine. The synagogue was adapted as a partial substitute for the Temple, and thus acquired even greater importance in Jewish life. Descriptions of the sacrifices were added to the liturgy, as the closest practical alternative to the sacrifices themselves. Several prayers previously recited in the Temple were transferred to the synagogue; and new prayers for the restoration of the Temple and for national redemption were added. The organization of the synagogue and its liturgy have remained relatively unchanged in their essentials from that time to the present day; and the synagogue still functions as a house of prayer and study, as well as a center of communal and social activity.

THE SYNAGOGUE BUILDING

The form of the synagogue building is governed by its original purposes – those of reading the Torah to the people, and of enabling them to participate in communal prayer. Basically, therefore, the synagogue consists of a room with seats for the worshippers, with a large bookcase of sorts in which the Torah scrolls are kept, and with a desk from which the Torah is read and from which the congregation may be led in prayer.

The Torah, or the Five Books of Moses, is handwritten on a parchment scroll called a SEFER (book or scroll – plural: SEFARIM). In earliest times the sacred scrolls were kept in a portable cupboard – or ARK – which was solemnly escorted in and out of the synagogue during the service. The Ark was always set down in the synagogue with its back facing the site of the Temple in Jerusalem. It was the focus of attention. In later years the use of a mobile Ark was discontinued, and the scrolls were kept permanently in a fixed Ark, placed against the wall of the building that backed towards the Temple. This determined the orientation of the synagogue building, and enabled the congregation to turn in prayer to face both the Ark and Jerusalem.

The other principal feature of the synagogue interior is the reading desk to which the Sefarim are escorted in procession from the Ark, and from which both the Torah is read and public prayers are directed. The desk is placed on a raised platform called the BIMAH (or TEBAH), large enough to accommodate several people, and often containing seats.

A separate pulpit is usually provided for the giving of sermons and addresses. A perpetual light burns constantly above the Ark, commemorating the eternal flame once maintained in the Temple. Special seats, apart from those of the other worshippers, are often installed for the Rabbi and for the synagogue's officers.

In most traditional synagogues the reading desk is sited in the center or towards the rear of the room, facing towards the Ark. This arrangement enhances the ceremonial aspect of the liturgy by providing a natural processional route round the synagogue when carrying the scrolls from and back to the Ark. The Torah is read, and the other parts of the service are recited from the midst of the assembled worshippers, giving a sense of participation to all present.

In non-traditional synagogues and temples, the Bimah is often situated directly in front the of the Ark, facing the congregation. To use a theatrical analogy, the effect is that of a proscenium stage, as opposed to the theater-in-the-round of the traditional arrangement. There is a loss of intimacy, especially in a large building, with the worshippers tending to

PLAN OF TYPICAL SYNAGOGUE

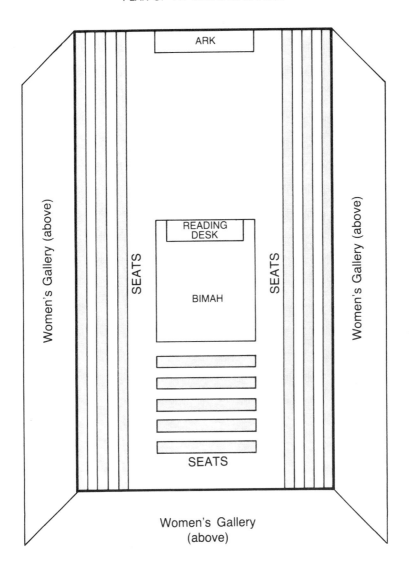

watch, rather than to participate in the proceedings.

Separation of men and women during worship is essential in all traditional synagogues. Some medieval buildings contained separate rooms for women, usually connected to the main hall by an aperture. Since the Renaissance women have usually been accommodated in galleries, built specially for the purpose as an integral part of the design. In early days the galleries were screened with heavy lattice work: later the screening became more symbolic than real. Many modern traditional synagogues seat men and women on the same level in different parts of the hall, achieving the required separation by means of light portable barriers.

Having lost its land in the year 70 C.E. the Jewish people was not able to develop an architectural style of its own in which to build synagogues. It was obliged to depend on the traditions and craftsmen of host countries, sometimes imitating the religious buildings of its neighbours, and sometimes doing its utmost to differ from them. Some synagogues are large and impressive: others are smaller and more intimate. Some synagogues are beautifully decorated and furnished: others, particularly those favored by very strictly observant Jews, are simple rooms with no adornment.

STATUTORY SERVICES

Three services are recited every day throughout the year, one in the morning, one in the afternoon and one in the evening. The core of each service is the prayer known as the AMIDAH. The presence of at least ten males over the age of thirteen is required for the public reading of the Amidah and for the public reading of the Torah.

SHAHRIT, the dawn or morning service, corresponds to the former morning sacrifice in the Temple. On Mondays and Thursdays (the ancient market days) and on Sabbaths and holy days a passage from the Torah is read. This is followed only on Sabbaths and holy days by the reading of a specially selected passage from the Prophets.

MINHA, the afternoon service, corresponds to the sacrifice that used to be offered at dusk in the Temple. On the afternoons of Sabbaths and fasts a passage from the Torah is also read, followed by one from the Prophets on fast days.

MA'ARIV (or ARVIT), the evening service, was originally regarded as optional by some authorities because it did not correspond to a former Temple sacrifice. When it was eventually decided to make its recital obligatory, the old doubt was reflected by having the Amidah said silently by the congregation only, and not also repeated aloud by the Reader, as in the other services.

On Sabbaths, new moons, festivals and the Day of Atonement, when an additional sacrifice was offered in the Temple, an additional service – MUSAF – is said in the synagogue directly after Shahrit, the morning service.

Yet another special service – NE'ILAH (closing) – is added at the conclusion of the Day of Atonement.

In practice, Shahrit and Musaf are recited together, one after the other, forming what is generally regarded as the Sabbath or holy day 'morning service' in the synagogue. Likewise, Arvit is very often said straight after Minha, thus enabling worshippers to fulfill both these obligations during a single visit to the synagogue in the early evening. Those unfamiliar with the liturgy, and unaware that they are participating in two entirely separate services, sometimes complain about what seems to them to be pointless repetition of some prayers, particularly the long Amidah.

STRUCTURE OF A SYNAGOGUE SERVICE

The proceedings in a modern synagogue differ little in their essentials from those in the distant past. The appropriate statutory services are recited, and passages from the Torah and the Prophets are read aloud to the people on certain specified occasions. Suitable dates have also been found for the inclusion in the synagogue liturgy of the five scrolls – the Books of Ruth, Esther, Ecclesiastes, Lamentations, and the Song of Songs. Inevitably, minor differences in liturgy and practice have arisen over the centuries between Ashkenazim and Sephardim, and between the numerous individual groups comprising those main categories.

The order of service on a Sabbath morning is very similar to that for the morning of a holy day. The structure of an ordinary Sabbath morning service is outlined below. Short descriptions of some of the main prayers are given later in this chapter.

Introduction to Shahrit

Proceedings start early in the morning with the recital of a selection of psalms and other passages designed to prepare the minds of the worshippers for what follows. Compared to a church, for example, the typical traditional synagogue is an informal place. Congregants tend to arrive at times to suit themselves, and mostly enter after the end of this particularly beautiful part of the service.

Shahrit (Morning Service)

The first part is centred round the Shema, which is set in a framework of verses, blessing and praising God and his works.

The Amidah is then said silently by the congregation, and is afterwards repeated out loud by the cantor. The ancient custom of repeating the Amidah arose for the benefit of those who knew little Hebrew and were unable to say this important prayer for themselves.

On holy days the biblical command to the sons of Aaron the High Priest to bless the people is fulfilled when those who by tradition claim descent from the House of Aaron – the COHANIM (plural of Cohen, priest) – go up to the Ark at the end of the Amidah prayer and bless the assembled congregation: 'May the Lord bless you and keep you....' The Cohanim first remove their shoes, and also publicly wash their hands with the assistance of all the Levites present.

On new moons and festivals the repetition of the Amidah is followed by the recital of Hallel (Psalms 113–18), special psalms of rejoicing and thanksgiving.

Sefer (Scroll)

This ceremony, during which the Sefer Torah (Scroll of the Law) is read out to the people, is a survival of what is probably the earliest recorded example in history of mass adult education. The whole Torah (Five Books of Moses: Genesis, Exodus, Leviticus, Numbers and Deuteronomy) is read, section by section, each week throughout the year; and every year the full cycle of readings is repeated anew. The content of these readings was considered to be so important in early times that a special attendant used to stand by the reading desk to translate the Hebrew into Aramaic, the everyday language of the people. That practice continued for many centuries before being discontinued. Most worshippers now have the benefit of English translations and rabbinic commentaries alongside the Hebrew text.

A Sefer Torah is a parchment scroll on which the entire Torah has been handwritten by a scribe. The writing is carried out with meticulous care, as the least error would render the scroll unfit for use. The text used is that of the oldest traditionally accepted version, with all later additions (including vowel signs) omitted. This does of course make it difficult to recite or chant a passage without careful rehearsal, as the Hebrew alphabet only comprises consonants, and has no vowels. Vowel signs, to aid reading, were added to the Hebrew letters in the fourth century C.E. Accents to indicate the traditional chants were added even later.

The reverence accorded to all aspects of the preparation of a Sefer Torah and its handling and reading arises directly from the belief that the scroll contains the very message transmitted by God, through Moses, to the Jewish people.

The scroll itself is mounted on wooden handles, for ease of rolling, unrolling, and carrying. It is covered by a richly embroidered mantle (or contained in a silver case). It may be crowned with a crown of precious metal or with ornamental bells, and clad with a 'breastplate'. A pointer in the form of a 'hand', to assist in the reading, is attached. Several scrolls, each elaborately dressed as just described, are kept in the Ark of most synagogues. One scroll is taken out for reading on weekdays and Sabbaths. On New Moons (when falling on a Sabbath) and holy days, two scrolls are used. These are carried to and from the reading desk with equal pomp.

The Sefer is removed from the Ark with great ceremony, and is carried in procession to the reading desk – quickly, as all are anxious to hear it read out – where it is reverently prepared for reading. At some stage in the proceedings it is partly unrolled and held up high to enable all the congregation to see the written words, and to pronounce a salutation.

The first worshipper chosen (this must be a Cohen if one is available) is called by Hebrew name to the reading desk; and the first portion of the weekly passage is read aloud on his behalf to the congregation, using the chant traditional for such reading. The second portion is read for a Levite, if one is present. The process is repeated with other Jews not descended from the Tribe of Levi until at least seven have been called. A lesser number is called on days other than Sabbaths. Originally each person read his own portion from the scroll; but this privilege is now restricted to relatively few people, such as a Bar Mitzvah or a distinguished rabbi.

The Sefer is then passed back to the bearer, who sits with it at the back of the Bimah while a lay member of the congregation stands at the reading desk and chants the weekly portion from the Prophets. Less ceremony is attached to this reading because, though all parts of the Hebrew Bible are considered to be sacred, only the Torah is regarded as having a wholly Divine origin.

The Sefer, clad in its full regalia, is held in the arms of the Rabbi who pronounces the prayer for the government (or for the King, Queen or President as appropriate), the prayer for the state of Israel, and the prayer for the congregation. The sacred scrolls are then escorted back to the Ark in solemn procession, slowly and lingeringly this time, while the congregation sings one of the Psalms of David.

Musaf (Additional Service)

This starts as soon as the Sefer has been returned to the Ark. The Amidah is said silently by the congregation, and is then repeated aloud by the Reader. Various other prayers follow, including ALENU, before which mourners say Kaddish. The morning ends with the well known hymns, EN KELOHENU (Who can be compared to our God) and ADON OLAM (Master of the World).

In traditional synagogues men and married women always keep their heads covered. Men (in some synagogues only married men) wear a Tallit (fringed prayer shawl) during the service. No organs, musical instruments or microphones are permitted on Sabbaths and holy days, as their use would be considered a form of 'work'. The choir, consisting of male voices only, simply leads the congregation in prayers and responses, and has no independent role. The sermon and the prayer for the government are delivered in English, but everything else is in Hebrew (except for the Kaddish, which is mostly Aramaic). Modern prayer books usually carry full English translations alongside the Hebrew texts. Women sit separately from the men and take no part in the public ceremonies. Jewish tradition assigns different roles to men and women. In fact women, unlike men, are not obliged to attend the statutory services in the synagogue at all, as it was recognized that other responsibilities would inhibit their presence at these long services: they are allowed therefore to pray at home in private. Though excluded from ceremonial, women can sometimes take an active part in other synagogue affairs by serving on committees, boards of management, and the like.

The practices followed in temples and most progressive synagogues contrast with those of the orthodox. Organs and microphones are widely used. Customs vary with regard to the covering of the head and the wearing of a Tallit, though the present tendency is veering towards the traditional. The English language is employed extensively in progressive and reform services, together with some Hebrew. The choir, comprising male and female voices, often sings set pieces on its own. Men and women sit together in synagogue during the service. And women very often share equally with the men in the ceremonial aspects of the worship.

THE RITUAL OF THE MITZVOT

These MITZVOT (literally 'commandments', but better translated as 'duties' in this particular context) connected with the synagogue service are the means by which individual worshippers may participate directly in the proceedings, and the means by which the whole congregation can share in the celebrations and sorrows of its individual members.

The mitzvot are mostly connected with the reading of the Torah. They are allotted by the President or Gabbai of the synagogue, who sits apart from the rest of the congregation and who accompanies the Sefer from the Ark to the reading desk where he remains until it is returned to the Ark. The principal mitzvot include the ceremonial opening and closing of the doors of the Ark, being called to the reading of the Torah, raising the opened Sefer to display it to the congregation, dressing the Sefer after the reading, and reading the Haftarah (portion from the Prophets). In Sephardi synagogues additional mitzvot are awarded, including reading Zemirot (Introduction to Shahrit), carrying the Sefer, accompanying the Sefer, and undressing the Sefer prior to the reading.

The bestowal of each mitzvah confers a degree of honor and recognition on the recipient. Local customs vary greatly concerning the different mitzvot and their suitability for different people. In general, age and learning are the qualities that are accorded the greatest recognition in the synagogue; and married men rank above bachelors. However, the mitzvot are also useful in encouraging the young to participate actively in the services.

Seven men are called to the reading of the Torah on an ordinary Sabbath, though more may be called on special occasions. This mitzvah is known as an ALIYAH (going-up). A Cohen is always called first, if available, thereby recognising the role of the descendants of the House of Aaron as the former priests and teachers of the people. A Levite is called next in acknowledgment of the supporting role of the tribe of Levi. The other aliyot are available for 'ordinary' Israelites, with the seventh slot (or the third in some congregations) considered to be the most honorific. Those qualifying for particular preference are a Bar Mitzvah, a bridegroom, a husband whose wife has just given birth, an engaged man, a mourner at the end of the thirty days of mourning, someone observing the anniversary of the death of a parent or very close relative, someone just recovered from a serious illness or returned from a dangerous journey, and visitors to the synagogue. Each man called may often make a public 'offering' to the synagogue or to related charities, if this is the local custom.

The reader of the Haftarah (portion from the Prophets) is selected from as wide a circle as possible, including the very young. A man observing the anniversary of the death of a parent may sometimes ask for this mitzvah.

The awarding of the mitzvot gives great scope for the weaving of strong personal and family elements into the fabric of each Sabbath and holy day service. A perceptive President or Gabbai can contribute significantly by these means to making his synagogue into a true center of communal life.

LITURGY

Although detailed discussion of the synagogue liturgy must lie beyond the scope of this book, outlines of several of its highlights are described in the following notes.

The Shema

Hear O Israel, the Lord is our God, the Lord is one.

And you shall love the Lord your God with all your heart, with all your soul and with all your might.

And these words which I command you this day shall be upon your heart; and you shall teach them diligently to your children, and shall talk of them when you sit in your house, when you walk by the way, when you lie down and when you rise up.

And you shall bind them for a sign on your hand, and they shall be for frontlets between your eyes. You shall write them on the doorposts of your house, and upon your gates.[2]

The Shema (hear) consists of three paragraphs from the Bible, the first of which (from the Book of Deuteronomy) is quoted in full above.

The Shema is regarded as the central confession of the Jewish faith. It is not a prayer as such, but an affirmation of the key principles of the religion. Its recitation formed a part of the daily service in the Temple, and was taken over by the synagogue when the Temple ceased to exist. The phrase 'when you lie down and when you rise up' is taken to mean that the Shema must be said early in the morning and late in the evening. It is therefore included in the morning and the evening services.

The first verse of the Shema,

SHEMA YISRAEL ADONAI ELOHENU, ADONAI EHAD
(Hear O Israel, the Lord is our God, the Lord is one),

is a statement of the fundamental belief in monotheism: there is only one God, the Creator of heaven and earth, and it is that God whom the Jews worship. The terseness of the Hebrew is difficult to translate into English, especially as the sentence employs one of the actual names of God, never pronounced outside the Temple, and now rendered as ADONAI (the Lord). The English version given above is the one most commonly accepted. These are the first Hebrew words taught to young Jewish children, before they are able to read; and they are very often the last words uttered before the moment of death. It is customary for some to cover the eyes with the right hand, or with the Tallit (prayer shawl), in order to achieve the utmost concentration when reading this verse during prayers.

The second verse, 'you shall love the Lord your God', teaches that belief in God, important though this may be, is insufficient in itself. Belief must always be accompanied by action; and this action is to serve God through love, with every fibre of one's being. In biblical times the heart was considered to be the seat of the intellect. The exhortation to love God is therefore intended to appeal to the intellect as well as to the emotions.

The next injunction of the Shema stresses the vital importance of teaching one's children to love and to serve God. Only by doing this can the Divine message be transmitted from generation to generation.

The remaining commands of the first paragraph are literally obeyed by observant Jews to this day. Tefillin (small leather boxes containing the written words of the Shema, and inaccurately translated as 'phylacteries') are strapped by men to the forehead and to the left arm (except for a left-handed person) for morning prayers (except on Sabbaths and festivals). A MEZUZAH (small box containing the written words of the Shema) is fixed to the front doorpost of Jewish homes and to each of the internal doorposts.

The next paragraph of the Shema, also from Deuteronomy, eloquently expresses the doctrine of reward and punishment in an agricultural and national context: 'If you observe My commandments with diligence . . . I will send the rain for your land in its due season . . . and you shall eat and be satisfied. . . .' Neglect of God's commandments, on the other hand, will lead to disaster: 'He will shut up the heavens, that there will be no rain . . . and you shall perish quickly off the good land which the Lord has given you.'

The paragraph continues by reiterating the obligations to love God, to teach children, and literally to display the precepts, so that 'Your days and the days of your children may be as long as the days of the heavens above the earth, in the land which the Lord promised to give your ancestors.'[3]

The last paragraph of the Shema, from the Book of Numbers, contains the command to the Israelites to wear fringes on the corners of their garments as a constant reminder of God's words: '. . . that you may look upon them and remember all the commandments of the Lord, and do them'.[4] This is the origin of the small fringed garment, Tsitsit, worn constantly by strictly observant Jews, and of the Tallit (prayer shawl) worn by men in the synagogue. The Shema ends with a final reminder of the covenant made with the Jewish people when God redeemed them from a life of slavery in Egypt: 'I am the Lord your God who brought you out of the land of Egypt to be your God: I am the Lord your God.'[4]

The Kaddish

Several variations of this ancient prayer are recited during each of the statutory synagogue services. The Kaddish is also said by mourners. A full explanation of the prayer, together with an English translation, will be found in the section on Death and Mourning.

The Amidah

The Amidah is the very core of each service in the synagogue, as mentioned earlier. The word Amidah means 'standing'; and the prayer was so named because, unlike the
Shema, it is always said standing. For many centuries the
prayer was simply known as the Tefillah (the Prayer), denot-
ing its prime importance. It is also known as the SHEMONEH-
ESREH (eighteen) because it once consisted of eighteen blessings, even though it now contains nineteen.

The prayer is of great antiquity, and parts are said to have
been compiled from more ancient sources, by Ezra and the
Men of the Great Assembly (about 400 B.C.E.). The first three
and the last three benedictions in their original forms date
from the early part of the second Temple period, and most of
the others are thought to be at least as old as the Maccabean
period. Though many of the actual words of the benedictions
have changed over the years, some of the original versions
were recited daily in the Temple together with the Shema
and the Ten Commandments. Scholars disagree as to whether
there were seventeen or eighteen (or even nineteen) benedictions when the form of the prayer finally crystallized in about
100 C.E. though such controversy is of academic interest only.
It now contains nineteen verses on weekdays, and is reduced
to seven verses on the Sabbath.

The Amidah is recited with the utmost concentration and
devotion. The worshipper stands with his feet together, facing
Jerusalem. He is addressing the Almighty directly in this
prayer and no distraction can be tolerated until it has been
completed. He will bow several times at appointed places,
acknowledging God's sovereignty. Before the prayer ends he
will step three short paces backwards, symbolizing his withdrawal from the Divine Presence.

After the silent recital of the Amidah by the congregation
during the Shahrit, Musaf and Minha services, the entire
prayer is repeated aloud by the Reader, with the congregation
responding in appropriate places. This practice was started
for the benefit of those who did not know the prayer, or else
knew insufficient Hebrew for them to say it for themselves. It
continues because of long-established custom, and also partly
for the original reasons, even though most worshippers are

now equipped with prayer books (including English translations). The Amidah is not repeated during the Arvit (or Maariv) service, in recognition of the fact that this service was once considered optional.

The Amidah's structure is carefully organized. The first three verses are blessings of praise to God, the following thirteen consist of petitions of various kinds, and the last three verses are expressions of thanks. On Sabbaths the middle thirteen benedictions are replaced by a single one of appreciation of the joys of the Sabbath, making seven in all. The prayer is too long to quote in full, and a brief description follows:

BENEDICTIONS:

1. God is adored as the God of the Patriarchs Abraham, Isaac and Jacob; and the hope is expressed that he will, in love, bring redemption to their descendants.
2. God is adored as the Supreme Power of the universe, the God of Nature, who also 'sustains the living with loving-kindness, resurrects the dead, supports the fallen, heals the sick, frees the captives and keeps faith with those who sleep in the dust'. It is thought that the specific reference to the resurrection was added by the Pharisees when this belief was disputed by the Sadducees.
3. God is adored for his holiness. In the repetition of the Amidah the congregation joins with the Reader in reciting the Kedusha (sanctification), starting with the formula said to be uttered daily by the angels who minister to the Divine Presence:
   Holy, holy, holy is the Lord of Hosts:
   the whole earth is full of His glory.
4. God is asked to favor us with knowledge (of good) and understanding.
5. God is asked to cause us to repent, and to draw near to His teaching.
6. God is asked to forgive us for our sins and transgressions.
7. God is asked to look on our afflictions and to redeem us from our sufferings. Spiritual and physical suffering is included here.

8. God is asked to heal the sick amongst us:
   Heal us O Lord, and we shall be healed. . .
9. God is asked to provide rain and dew in their seasons and to bless the land with abundant harvests.
10. God is asked to gather the exiles of the Jewish people 'from the four corners of the earth'.
11. God is first asked to restore our judges as in former times (i.e. to restore the rule of Divine Law); and the prayer then becomes one for universal redemption, when he will reign over all mankind in loving-kindness, mercy and righteousness.
12. God is asked to punish the slanderers against his people and to 'humble and uproot the dominion of arrogance'. This petition was added by Rabbi Gamliel round about 100 C.E. against sectarians and heretics. The text was altered several times at the insistence of Christian censors, who interpreted it as a prayer against them. The word 'slanderers' presently used in the text refers to converted Jews who informed on their former brethren, and caused them to be persecuted.
13. God is asked to reward the pious members of the community, and the true converts to Judaism in its midst. This was added in praise of the righteous community established as the result of the Maccabean revolt in 165 B.C.E.
14. God is asked to rebuild Jerusalem and the Temple.
15. God is asked to restore the Royal House of David and to hasten the coming of the Messiah.
16. God is asked to hear and to accept our prayers. Personal petitions may be added by the worshipper at this point.
17. God is asked to restore the Temple ritual and his worship in general. This is one of the oldest parts of the Amidah, derived from the prayer of thanks for God's worship that was recited daily in the Temple.
18. God is thanked for his unfailing mercies, and for the good that he bestows each day.
19. God is asked to grant us peace and blessing. In the repetition of the prayer, God is asked to bless us with the three-fold blessing with which the priests were commanded to bless the people:

May the Lord bless you and keep you.
May the Lord cause His face to shine upon you and
be gracious unto you.
May the Lord look kindly on you and give you peace.

It must be stressed that these bare descriptions of the sense
of each verse cannot do justice to the beauty and power of
the original text, which readers are urged to experience for
themselves.

Alenu

This is another of the most ancient prayers in the liturgy. It
was originally recited in the Musaf service for the New Year,
and is now used to conclude each of the statutory daily
services. Medieval Christian censorship wrought havoc with
this prayer and compelled the deletion of passages referring
to idol-worshippers, even though the Jews maintained that
these referred to pagans, and not to Christians or Moslems.
The prayer is now recited in full once again, with Ashkenazi
and Sephardi versions differing.

The prayer is a testimony to God's rule over his people
Israel, and over the entire world. It ends with the messianic
hope that the Lord will be acknowledged as King over all the
earth:

It is our duty to praise the Lord of all things, to ascribe
greatness to Him who formed the world in the
beginning. . . . We prostrate ourselves and worship the
supreme King of kings, the Holy One, blessed he He . . .
He is our God, and there is none else . . . (Sephardim end
here).

We therefore hope . . . that we may see the glory of Your
might when You will remove all abominations from the
earth. . . . Let all the inhabitants of the earth know and
realise that to You every knee shall bend. . . . Let them all
accept the yoke of Your kingdom . . . and the Lord shall
be King over all the earth; in that day shall the Lord be
one, and His name one.[5]

PERSONNEL

Priest

Since the destruction of the Temple in 70 C.E. there has been no very meaningful role for the hereditary priesthood. Only vestiges of its original authority and privilege survive today, when the sole public task remaining for the descendants of the House of Aaron – the Cohanim (priests) – is to bless the assembled congregation at certain fixed times in obedience to the command contained in the Book of Numbers: 'May the Lord bless you and keep you...' Descendants of the Tribe of Levi – the Levites – whose ancestors once officiated in the Temple, assist the Cohanim to wash their hands before pronouncing the blessing.

Rabbi

The Bible describes how Moses conferred leadership on Joshua by laying hands upon him. Moses also ordained seventy Elders in similar manner to assist him in judging and ruling the people; and those Elders ordained others in their turn. The Talmud relates that this system of ordination, known as SEMIHA (laying) continued in unbroken line from the time of Moses to that of the second Temple. The chain was finally broken some centuries later, on the decline of the Palestinian academies. The modern form of Semiha originated in the Middle Ages, when it became a diploma conferred by a rabbi on his pupil. It recognized the pupil's scholarship and gave him the title of 'rabbi', thereby enabling him to act as a judge and teacher of the people. These days the Semiha is usually granted to a student by a Yeshiva (theological college) or similar institution. It can, however, still be bestowed on his pupil by a single rabbi – its status depending very much on the learning and authority of the teacher.

The rabbi is the traditional judge and teacher. He is not a priest as such, though he may coincidentally also be a Cohen (priest). Jewish law embraces all aspects of criminal, civil and religious jurisdiction. In ancient times therefore the Rabbi and the Beth Din (rabbinic court) were the only valid legal authorities, with the power of life and death. These functions continued in autonomous and semi-autonomous Jewish communities throughout the Middle Ages, though rabbis no longer exercised capital powers after the breaking of the original chain of ordination. In modern times, with the over-all jurisdiction of secular (non-Jewish) law in western countries, the legal work of a rabbi is mostly confined to religious matters and to questions of personal status such as conversion, marriage and divorce. The present function of a rabbi is now mainly that of interpreting and teaching Jewish tradition, of guiding and preaching to the people, and (since the last century) of acting in much the same way as a Christian minister or pastor.

Earlier generations of rabbis were not paid, and earned their living from other sources: Maimonides (twelfth century), for example, practised as a physician. It was then considered wrong to derive financial benefit from studying or teaching the Torah, a view which is still maintained in certain quarters. An early account of a paid rabbinic appointment comes from the fourteenth century, when in order to enable a penniless refugee to take up a position of Rabbi of a community, it was arranged that he should be paid 'compensation' for his resulting inability to maintain himself by other means. Rabbis are now almost always paid officials of the synagogues to which they are attached.

Until the nineteenth century Jewish tradition had no precise equivalent to the Christian minister or pastor. However in most modern synagogues the Rabbi - or the Hazan, if there is no rabbi - undertakes a pastoral role in addition to his traditional duties of interpreting and teaching the Torah and guiding the people. He is expected to educate the young, organize the old, counsel the perplexed, spearhead charitable activities, visit the sick, comfort the mourners, and perform marriages and funerals, as well as conducting parts of the regular synagogue services.

The emergence of a paid clerical profession to take over tasks once performed by laymen owes a good deal to outside influences. Most people think that the system accords reasonably well with modern needs; though it must remain an open question as to whether or not the Jewish 'ministry' provides adequate religious leadership.

HAZAN (Cantor)

The custom has become established in larger synagogues of employing specially trained professional cantors to enhance the beauty of the singing and chanting. In England, the Hazan is usually accorded the courtesy title of 'Reverend'; in a congregation without a Rabbi, he may act as its spiritual leader.

Any religiously observant Jew is permitted to conduct any part of the synagogue service – including the reading from the Sefer Torah (Scroll of the Law), if competent to do so. Thus the recital of a typical traditional service is usually shared between the Cantor and several skilled laymen. If there is a Rabbi, he will also take part.

SYNAGOGUE OFFICERS

The Officers of the Congregation, specially elected by the members to direct its affairs, usually sit in prominent seats apart from the other worshippers.

The title of the officer whose task it is to allot the mitzvot, and in Spanish and Portuguese synagogues to 'preside' over the services, varies in accordance with local custom. He is often called the GABBAI, but may also be known as the President, the Parnas or the Warden. He will accompany the Sefer Torah to the reading desk, and will stand there while it is being read. Other members of the Ritual Committee sometimes serve as voluntary ushers.

In Reform synagogues the Rabbi conducts the entire service himself. It is still usual for the President (or Gabbai) to allot the mitzvot, but he seldom sits in a special seat or stands at the reading desk (Bimah).

SHAMASH (Ritual Director)

The Officers, who all serve in an honorary capacity, may be assisted in the ritual logistics of using the synagogue for public prayer by a paid official called a SHAMASH, a Ritual Director, or a Sexton. The Ritual Director also works with the Rabbi and the Cantor as a member of the pastoral team.

A Sexton is not usually employed in Reform synagogues, the work he would have done being shared by the Committee members on a voluntary basis.

SYNAGOGUE TYPES

Since the destruction of the Temple, Jews have lived in many countries of the world, always in exile and often fearful of the next catastrophe which may lie ahead. In modern times the Russian pogroms of the late nineteenth century drove vast numbers of people away from the lands in which they had lived for hundreds of years. The rise and fall of Nazi Germany sent the survivors of the holocaust scurrying for shelter throughout the world; and the recent rise of Arab nationalism, coupled with the birth of the State of Israel, has resulted in the almost complete dispersion of the many ancient Jewish communities of the Near East.

Yearning for some kind of stability many Jews have been conservative in their religious lives, resisting change. Each separate group has tended to hark back with nostalgia to the customs established in the particular golden age during which its own ancestors were able to flourish for a while in peace and tranquility. For example, the sixteenth-century Polish-Jewish costume (then modelled partly on the former dress of the Polish nobility, and partly on Persian styles) is still worn today by the strictly observant heirs of the old East European traditions. Congregations of Spanish and Portuguese Jews still use Portuguese words and titles in their synagogues, almost four hundred years after the expulsion of the Jews from Portugal. It may be amusing to recall that the proposal to clad their ministers in the Victorian top hats commonly worn by the ordinary members of the congregation – in place of the then traditional three-cornered hats – caused a schism within the London Sephardim in 1879, and provoked many to break away from their parent synagogue. Groups of relatively recent immigrants tend to cling even more tenaciously to the music and customs of their 'native' lands.

It is not surprising therefore that synagogues vary in atmosphere and tone as greatly as did the groups of people who originally established them in answer to their own special needs. Though not differing in any of the essentials of the worship, it can hardly be expected, for example, that the music developed in the Jewish communities of Iraq will sound anything like that developed in the cities of Germany: nor will the courtly manners of the Spanish Jews closely resemble those of Jews from the agricultural villages of Poland. Though there are only small variations to the principal prayers in the Ashkenazi and the Sephardi rites, subsidiary passages that do not come directly from the Bible or Talmud are often different. Ashkenazi prayer books depend heavily on the work of Kallir, who lived in Palestine possibly towards the end of the sixth century: Sephardi liturgy, on the other hand, is enriched by the compositions of the poets of the Spanish golden age, such as Ibn Gabirol and Yehuda Halevi.

The choice of a synagogue will usually be governed by upbringing and family custom, though ultimately it is a matter of personal taste. The rich diversity of available styles can be both fascinating and stimulating. Some will be attracted to the small 'shtibl' or prayer house of the more strictly observant Jews, and will delight in its atmosphere of friendliness and extreme informality – while others will be repelled by its apparent hubbub and confusion. Many will gravitate towards the large synagogues of the mainstream Ashkenazi community, finding that this particular blend of 'meeting place' and 'prayer house' answers well to their religious and social needs – others will be irritated by the constant chatter during the services, and yet others will object equally strongly to the lack of intimacy. Some will appreciate the dignity of the Spanish and Portuguese synagogues – but those very qualities may also arouse dislike. Non-traditional Jews and families with mixed religious heritage may opt for the often lavish houses of worship of the Conservative, Reform or Reconstructionist movements. Their church-like decorum, choir, mixed seating, musical instruments and partly English language liturgy will comfort some, just as it bothers others. To summarize, a wide diversity of synagogues exists, fully reflecting the richness of world-wide Jewish traditions.

List of Quotations

ABBREVIATIONS

A.D.P.B. Authorised Daily Prayer Book of the United Hebrew
Congregations of the British Commonwealth
(*Singer's Prayer Book*).
S. & P. Prayer Books of the Spanish and Portuguese Jews,
London.

INTRODUCTION

[1]Num. 24:5
[2]Jer. 2:2

1: BIRTH

[1]Gen. 17:10–12
[2]Spinoza, *Tractatus Theologico-Politicus*, 3:53
[3]Num. 6:22–6

2: BAR MITZVAH AND BAT MITZVAH

[1]Num. 6:22–6

3: MARRIAGE

[1]Gen. 18:24
[2]A.D.P.B. and S. & P.
[3]Talmud (B): Yebamoth 20a
[4]Genesis. Rabbah 9:7
[5]Prov. 31:10–25
[6]Prov. 31:30
[7]Gen. 29:20
[8]Song of Songs 8:6–13
[9]A.D.P.B. and S. & P.

[10]Lev. 19:2
[11]Exod. 19:6
[12]Gen. 1:28

4: DEATH AND MOURNING

[1]Eccles. 12:5
[2]Eccles. 3:1–4
[3]S. & P.
[4]Job 1:21
[5]Job 3:2
[6]Job 38:4
[7]A.D.P.B. and S. & P.
[8]Eccles. 12:7
[9]Gen. 1:27
[10]Gen. 37:34
[11]S. & P.
[12]Job 1:21
[13]Ecclus. 38:16–17
[14]Ecclus. 38:20–1
[15]Gen. 50:10
[16]Num. 20:29

5: CONCEPTS

[1]Exod. 3:14
[2]Talmud (P): Hagigah 1:7
[3]Exod. 34:6–7
[4]Lev. 19:2
[5]Lev. 19:3
[6]Lev. 19:12
[7]Mic. 6:8
[8]Ethics of the Fathers, included in A.D.P.B.
[9]Job 31:13–15
[10]Mishnah Makkot 1:10
[11]Talmud (B): Shabbat 31a
[12]Lev. 19:18
[13]Num. 15:15–16
[14]Job 31:28–9
[15]Sifre Zutra: Num. 18
[16]A. Pope, Second Epistle of the 'Essay on Man'
[17]Ps. 49:12
[18]Ps. 8:6–10
[19]S. & P.
[20]Talmud (B): Sotah 14a

[21]Maimonides: Thirteen Principles of Faith, included in A.D.P.B. and in S. & P.
[22]Zech. 14:9
[23]Maimonides: Thirteen Principles of Faith, included in A.D.P.B. and in S. & P.
[24]Talmud (B): Berachot 17a
[25]Gen. 12:1–2
[26]Exod. 19:6
[27]W. N. Ewer and another.
[28]Exod. 19:5
[29]Tosefta: Sanhedrin 13
[30]Ps. 137:1–6

6: TORAH

[1]Talmud (B): Menahoth 29b
[2]Gen. 8:11
[3]Genesis Rabbah 33:6
[4]Benjamin of Tudela: from J. R. Marcus, *The Jew in the Mediaeval World*. New York, 1960.
[5]Maimonides: from *Letters of the Jews through the Ages*, I, ed. F. Kobler (East and West Library, 1952)

7: KABBALAH

[1]Ethics of the Fathers, included in A.D.P.B.

8: THE JEWISH YEAR

[1]Gen. 2:1–3
[2]Exod. 20:8–11
[3]Gen. 1:31
[4]Deut. 16:16
[5]Exod. 12:14
[6]Passover Haggadah
[7]Passover Haggadah
[8]Exod. 12:15
[9]Exod. 12:34
[10]Exod. 12:39
[11]S. & P.
[12]Exod. 19:4–5
[13]Exod. 19:16
[14]Deut. 34:10
[15]Song of Songs 4:11
[16]Lev. 23:42–3

[17]Lev. 23:39–40
[18]Amidah for the New Year, A.D.P.B. and S. & P.
[19]S. & P.
[20]Eccles. 9:7

9: THE HOME

[1]A.D.P.B. and S. & P.
[2] Gen. 1:29
[3]Lev. 7:26–7
[4]Gen. 32:33
[5]Deut. 14:21
[6]Exod. 22:30
[7]Lev. 20:26
[8]Genesis Rabbah 44:1

10: THE SYNAGOGUE

[1]Num. 6:22–6
[2]Deut. 6:4–9
[3]Deut. 11:13–21
[4]Num. 15:37–41
[5]A.D.P.B. and S. & P.

Further Reading

THE AGES OF MAN

Jewish Medical Ethics, I. Jakobovits (New York 1959 and subsequent editions)
A Guide to Life, H. Rabinowicz (London 1969)
Birth Control in Jewish Law, D. M. Feldman (London 1968)
Contemporary Halachic Problems, J. D. Bleich (New York 1983)
Jewish Life in the Middle Ages, I. Abrahams (New York 1961)

THE FRAMEWORK OF BELIEF

Judaism, A Historical Presentation, I. Epstein (London 1970)
A Book of Jewish Thoughts, J. Herz (Oxford 1921)
A History of the Jewish People, H. H. Ben Sasson (London 1976)
The Jew in the Modern World, P. R. Mendes-Flohr (Oxford 1980)
A History of Mediaeval Jewish Philosophy, I. Husik (Philadelphia 1958)
Everyman's Talmud, A. Cohen (New York 1975)
Hebrew Ethical Wills, I. Abrahams (Philadelphia 1926)
Major Trends in Jewish Mysticism, G. Scholem (New York 1941)
Ashkenazim and Sephardim, H. J. Zimmels (London 1958)

THE FRAMEWORK OF OBSERVANCE

Guides to the Jewish Festivals (separate volumes published in a set by Jewish Chronicle Publications, London)
Annotated Edition to the Authorised Daily Prayer Book, I. Abrahams (London 1914)
The Jewish Dietary Laws, I. Grunfeld (London 1972)
The Synagogue, B. de Breffny (London 1978)

Index

Page numbers in bold refer to main entries

Abortion 35
Arraham 10, 16, 65, 68, 79, 83, 88
Abstention from sex 21, 34, 146
Adam, the first man 76, 121
Adam Kadmon 120
Additional Service 157, 160, 166
Afternoon Service 156
Aggadah 90, 98, 106, 108
Akiva, Rabbi 6, 72, 73, 87, 93, 94, 142
Albo, Joseph **66**, 69
Alenu prayer, 160, **169**
Alfasi (Rabbi Isaac of Fez) 102, 104
Aliyah (in synagogue) 18, 162
Amidah prayer 153, 158, 160, **166**
Amoraim **96**, 98, 104
Amulets 111
Anniversery of death 59
Aramaic, language 28, 50, 90, 96, 159
Ark of the synagogue **154**, 160, 162
Artificial insemination 9
Arvit - see Evening Service
Asheri (Rabbi Asher ben Yehiel) 103, 104
Ashkenazim **4**, 102, 104, 115, 174

Ba'al Shem Tov, the (Israel ben Eliezer) 107, **116**
Babylon 4, 84, 90, 96, 99, 151
Bar Mitzvah 18, 19
Bastard 15
Bat Mitzvah 17, 19
Beth Din - see Court, rabbinic
Betrothal 29, 30
Bible 65, 89, 99
Bill of divorce 36

Bimah of the synagogue 154
Birth **9**
Blessings, special 145
Breaking of the vessels 123
Bride 27, 28, 29
Burial 41, 45

Calendar 18, 59, 129, 130
Cantor 172
Caro, Joseph 84, **104**, 125
Celibacy - see Abstention from sex
Christianity, the Church 2, 79, 81, 83, 113, 116, 132, 152, 169
Chosen people 79
Chuppah - see Wedding canopy
Circumcision 10
Coffin **44**
Cohen 13, 60, 158, 160, **162**, 170
Conservative Judaism 5
Contraception 33
Conversion, converts 14, 80, **82**, 107
Court, rabbinic 11, 24, 35, 75, 105
Creation 111, 118, 122, **131**, 140
Cremation 44
Crusades 51, 83, 100

David, King 77, 80, 168
Day of Atonement 48, 139, **141**, 151
Day of Judgment 78
Days of Awe 139
Death penalty 72
Derasha 19
Dew, prayer for 136
Dietary laws 23, **147**
Divine Chariot 111
Divine names 110
Divorce 22, 24, 28, **35**, 105

El Male Rahamim prayer - see Memorial Prayer
Elijah 10, 11, 113
England 101
En-Sof 117, 118, 122
Ethics, Jewish 65, **70**, 112
Etrog 138
Evening service 157
Evil 66, 68, 110, **121**, 123
Euthanasia 61
Exilarch 96, 99
Ezra 90, 153, 166

Fasts, fasting 27, 60, 141, 143
Five Books of Moses - see Torah
Flowers at funerals 45
Forgiveness of sins 141
Funeral - see Burial

Gabbai of synagogue - see Warden
Garden of Eden - see Paradise
Gehinam - see Hell
Gemara **96**, 98
Genizah 98
Gentiles 73, **81**
Geonim 98, 105
Germany 4, 69, 112
Gershon, Rabbi 23, 100, 105
Get 36
Gilgul - see Reincarnation
Godfather - see Sandak
Grace after meals 145

Haftarah 18, 160, 162
Halachah 69, **90**, 92, 108
Hallel psalms 74, **152**, 158
Hanukah 142
Hashkabah prayer - see Memorial Prayer
Hasidim, E. European movement 109, **116**
Hasidim, medieval German movement 112
Hazan - see Cantor
Heaven - see Paradise
Hebrew language 1, 4, 90, 95, 99, 100, 112, 159, 161
Hell 78
Hevra Kadisha - see Holy Brotherhood

Hillel 34, 72, **92**, 105
Holy Brotherhood 43

Ibn Gabirol 69, 174
Illegitimacy 15
Immortality of the soul **76**, 92
Isaac 65, 79, 140
Islam 4, 79, 81, 99, 132
In-vitro fertilization 9
Israel, land of 82
Israel, state of 79, 83, 85, 160
Isserles, Rabbi Moses 104

Jabneh 93
Jacob 16, 25, 65, 79, 83, 148
Job 40, 52, 55, 71, 89
Judah the Prince 94

Kabbalah 6, 53, 101, **109**
Kaddish prayer 47, **50**, 55, 58, 59, 161, 165
Kal Nidre prayer 141
Kallir 174
Karaite movement 100
Kashering meat 148
Kashrut - see Dietary laws
Kedusha 167
Keriah - see Rending of garments
Ketubah - see Marriage contract
Kiddush 132, 146
Kippah - see Skull cap

Lag ba'Omer 142
Lavadores - see Holy Brotherhood
Law, the - see Halachah, and Torah
Leap year 130
Leon, Moses de 113
Levy, Levite 152, 158, 162, 170
Lulav 138
Lunar month 129, 130
Luria, Isaac 84, **114**, 122

Ma'Ariv - see Evening service
Maimonides, Moses 69, 76, 81, **102**, 104, 107, 171
Mamzer 15
Marriage ceremony 29
Marriage contract 24, **28**, 31
Masoretic text of the Bible 100
Matzah - see Unleavened bread

Meal of Consolation 55
Memorial candle 55, 60
Memorial stone 59
Memorial prayer **48**, 59
Menstruation 32
Merkabah 111
Messiah, Messianic Age 50, 51, **77**, 85, 110, 114, 115, 168
Mezuzah 165
Midrash **90**, 98
Mikveh - see Ritual bath
Milk and meat, separation of 148
Minha - see Afternoon service
Minyan 11, 16, 145, 156
Mishnah 91, 92
Mishnah, the **94**, 96
Mishneh Torah, the 103
Mitzvah 124, 144
Mitzvot in synagogue 161
Mohel 11
Monotheism **67**
Month - see Lunar month
Moon, the 129
Moral code 67, 70, 71
Morning service 18, **156**, **158**
Moses 65, 70, 76, 87, 89, 135, 137, 170
Moslems - see Islam
Mourning 39, **54**, 58
Musaf - see Additional service
Mysticism 5, **110**

Nahalah - see Anniversary of death
Naming a boy 12
Naming a girl 13
Ne'ilah **141**, 157
New Moon **133**, 157
New Year 139, **140**
Noachide laws 81
Noah 81, 90
Nuptials 29, 31

Onan 34
Onen 42
Oral Law 89, 91, 106, **111**
Oral Torah - see Oral Law
Ordination, rabbinic - see Semiha

Paradise 78

Parve food 148
Passover 130, 134, **135**
Pentcost - see Shavuot
Pharisees 92
Philo 69
Philosophy 68
Phylacteries - see Tefillin
Pidyon-ha-Ben - see Redemption
Poland 104, 115
Polygamy 23, 105
Portion from the Prophets - see Haftarah
Practical Kabbalah 110
Prayer shawl - see Tallit
Pre-existence of souls - see Immortality of the soul
President of synagogue - see Warden
Priest - see Cohen
Priestly blessing 152, 158, 168
Procreation 33
Progressive Judaism - see Reform Judaism
Prophets 80, 89, 157, 160
Purim 142

Quorum, religious - see Minyan
Rabbenu Tam (Rabbi Jacob ben Meir) **101**, 105
Rabbi - see Judah the Prince
Rabbi, the 170
Rain, prayer for 139
Rambam - see Maimonides
Ram's Horn - see Shofar
Rashi (Rabbi Shelomo Itzhaki) **100**, 105
Rav (Abba Arika) 96
Reconstructionist Judaism 5
Redemption of the first born 12
Reform Judaism **4**
Reform Judaism, practices differing from Orthodox 4, 5, 20, 37, 44, 45, 47, 82, 134, 154, 172
Registrar for Births & Deaths 42
Registrar for Marriages 26
Reincarnation of souls 77, 122
Rending of garments 45
Responsa 99, **105**
Restoration - see Tikkun

Resurrection of the dead 78
Reverend, the 172
Ritual bath 26, 32
Ritual Director - see Shamash
Ritual slaughter 75, **147**
Rosh, the - see Asheri
Rosh Hashanah - see New Year
Rosh Hodesh - see New Moon
Ruth 80, 137, 157

Sa'adia Gaon 69, 100, 140
Sabbath, the 18, 21, 27, 39, 54, 59,
    91, 107, **131**, 153, 158, 167
Sadducees 92
Safed 84, 114
Sandak 11
Sanhedrin 72, 93, 94
Scribes, the 90
Seder, Passover **136**, 146
Sefer Hasidim 112
Sefer Torah **154**, 159
Sefer Yetzirah 112
Sefirot, the 112, 118
Semiha 170
Sephardim **4**, 102, 173
Sex, sex drive 22, 28, 32, 146
Sexton of Synagogue - see Shamash
Shahrit - see Morning service
Shammai 92
Shamash of synagogue 172
Shavuot 134, **136**
Shechinah 119, 120, 123
Shehitah - see Ritual slaughter
Sheloshim 58
Shema, the 18, 152, 158, **163**
Shemoneh-Esreh - see Amidah
Shivah 54
Shofar 140, 141
Shohet 147
Sholem, Gershon 109, 113
Shulhan Aruch 104, 107
Skull cap 146
Sorcery 111
Soul, the 53, 76, 121
Spain 69, 100, 109, 115
Speculative Kabbalah 110
Statutory services 42, 55, **156**
Succot - see Tabernacles
Suicide 60

Sun, the 129
Surrogate mothers 9
Synagogue, the 2, **151**

Tabernacles, Feast of 134, **138**
Taharah 43
Tallit 43, 161, **165**
Talmud, the 2, 68, 70, 84, **95**, 97,
    99, 101
Tannaim, the **92**, 104
Tebah - see Bimah
Tefillah - see Amidah
Tefillin 18, 145, **164**
Ten Commandments 65, 132, 137,
    152
Ten Days of Penitence 139
Temple, the 83, 85, 93, 137, 138,
    140, 141, 143, 152, 153, 154,
    168
Tikkun 121, 124
Tisha be'Av 143
Tombstone - see Memorial stone
Torah, the 65, 70, 72, 79, 82, 84,
    87, 104, 136, 137
Tosafot 101
Transmigration of souls - see Rein-
    carnation
Tree of Divine Power - 119, 120
Tu Bi-Shevat 142
Tur, the 103
Tzaddic 116
Tzitzit 145, **165**

Unleavened bread 135

Warden of synagogue 172
Wedding canopy 27, 29, 30
Wedding dress 27
Wedding ring 27
Week, the 130
Women, in ritual 17, 53, 156, 160,
    161
Women's rights, in law 23, 24, 28,
    89

Yahrzeit - see Anniversary
Year of mourning 58
Yehudah the Hasid 112
Yeshivot 98, 170

Yiskor - see Memorial prayer
Yochai, Shimon bar 94, 113, 142
Yom ha-Azmaut 143
Yom Kippur - see Day of
   Atonement
Yom Yerushalayim 143

Zakkai, Jochanan ben 93
Zionism, political 83
Zohar, the **113**, 118, 120
Zvi, Shabbetai 109, **115**, 125